which?
essential guides

BUYING
PROPERTY
ABROAD

D0413369

" As exciting and financially lucrative as it may seem, the overseas property market is a minefield. This book will help you steer your way through it. **"**

Jeremy Davies

About the author

Jeremy Davies, a freelance journalist since 1990, has written about overseas property since 2003. He has contributed to a range of national newspapers, magazines, TV and radio shows, including *The Guardian, Homes Overseas, Dispatches* and *File on Four.*

essential guides

BUYING
PROPERTY
ABROAD

JEREMY DAVIES

This book is for Albert Sowerby Davies

Which? Books are commissioned and published by
Which? Ltd, 2 Marylebone Road, London, NW1 4DF
Email: books@which.co.uk

Distributed by Littlehampton Book Services Ltd
Faraday Close, Durrington, Worthing, West Sussex
BN13 3RB

British Library Cataloguing in Publication Data
A catalogue record for this book is available from the British Library

Copyright ©Which? Ltd 2006

ISBN 1 84490 024 X / 978 184490 024 4

Although the author and publishers endeavour to make sure the information in
this book is accurate and up-to-date, it is only a general guide. Before taking
action on financial, legal, or medical matters you should consult a qualified
professional adviser, who can consider your individual circumstances. The author
and publishers can not accordingly accept liability for any loss or damage
suffered as a consequence of relying on the information contained in this guide.

Author's acknowledgements
Jeremy Davies would like to thank Blevins Franks, Conti Financial Services, HM
Revenue and Customs, John Howell & Co, Needanadviser.com and the Royal
Institution of Chartered Surveyors, for useful background information; and Paolo
Barbieri for research assistance.

Editorial/design/production: Ian Robinson, Angela Newton, Paula Lock at
Which? Books; Guy Croton, Neil Adams, Vanessa Townsend at Focus Publishing

Cover photographs by: Getty/Photolibrary
Printed and bound by Scotprint, Scotland

Contents

Introduction

Millions of British expatriates live and work, or enjoy their retirement, abroad - and at any given time thousands more are making preparations to join them. In recent years the number of people in the UK who own a second property overseas, whether for use as a holiday home or as a buy-to-let investment, has grown enormously.

The TV shows that have helped fuel our obsession with overseas property make buying abroad look easy. But in reality, finding, purchasing and owning overseas can be a time-consuming business, and turning a foreign property into a successful investment can be even more of a struggle.

A growing market

Since the stock market crash at the end of the 20th century, Britain's longstanding fascination with bricks and mortar has intensified, and we have been casting our nets increasingly wide, in the search for ever-more exotic and profitable overseas homes.

Housing experts suggest lots of reasons for this. Household incomes are rising. Transport costs are falling. Consumer goods that enable us to live 'dual centre' lives are becoming cheaper. Increasing EU integration means we now have the right to live and buy property in other European countries. Eurozone mortgage rates are low. Perhaps most importantly, many of us have sufficient equity in our UK homes to fund the purchase of a second home overseas.

As a result, a whole new global industry has developed, offering UK-based overseas property hunters everything from estate agency, legal services and mortgage advice to lettings management, second home insurance, holiday home advertising and relocation services.

Estate agents and developers from around the world vie for custom at overseas property exhibitions in hotels and conference centres around Britain every weekend. News stands groan under the weight of magazines packed with advertisements featuring the latest luxury developments. Overseas property investment 'gurus' run costly seminars to share the secret of their success.

Buyer, beware!

STOP! If you are considering buying overseas, it is vital to be clear that absolutely everyone you encounter along the way has a vested interest in you sailing through the buying process and signing on the dotted line, regardless of whether the property meets your needs or whether you can afford such a financial commitment.

Estate agents want you to buy so they can earn their commission. Property management companies want the contract to look after your property. Even your lawyer, whom you are employing to give you impartial advice on how best to handle the purchase, needs you to go ahead with the purchase in order to earn his or her fee.

If you are borrowing to buy abroad, your mortgage broker or lender will look carefully at affordability, and may even enquire as to whether you have insurance to cover the extra loan repayments if you were to lose your job or were no longer able to work.

Plenty of borrowers massage the truth about their income and outgoings at this point, and make hollow promises that they will sort out income protection insurance - but the broker still goes away having earned their fee, and the lender has the security of knowing it could repossess your UK or overseas home if you default on the loan.

Getting it right

Only you can decide if you want to risk overstretching yourself. No matter how cheap an overseas property may first appear, it will almost certainly represent one of the biggest financial commitments of your life - and there will be no-one to sue if hoped-for

rental yields and capital growth do not arise. Do as much research as possible on the local property market, and always bear in mind that markets for second homes are generally the most volatile.

Failing to commission adequate property surveys, apply for the proper planning permissions and take proper legal advice can leave you vulnerable, so make such issues an absolute priority from the start. Some people have risked their whole life savings and jeopardised their future financial wealth by not taking adequate precautions, for example buying in areas where ownership disputes are common.

This book will be a vital tool in your armoury, helping you to:

- Decide whether you can afford to buy in the first place.
- Find the right property.
- Negotiate a contract that protects your interests.
- Deal with the authorities in the country you buy in, and back home.
- Enjoy your new property.
- When the time comes, sell quickly and at the right price.

Get all this right and you could have a wonderful new asset which gives you and your family enormous enjoyment over the years, and greater wealth in the long run. Get it wrong and you could be risking a good chunk of your future security on a pipe dream.

The top 10 pitfalls of overseas property buying

1. Overstretching your finances
Don't jump on the overseas property bandwagon unless you're sure why you're doing it, and that you can afford it – especially if you're securing it against your UK home.

2. Buying sight unseen
If you buy an overseas property without ever having seen it - and surprising numbers of people do - you've only got yourself to blame if it ends up being a disaster.

3. Buying without a lawyer
Lawyers may seem to make the process complicated, but the work they do is vital to protect your best interests - for example, telling you whether the seller has the legal right to sell. Pay extra for one who speaks good English and is qualified in UK and foreign law.

4. Failing to check credentials
Is the seller really the property owner? Is your estate agent really a qualified agent, and are they bonded to hold a deposit on your behalf? What guarantees are there if the developer goes bust?

5. Putting deposit down too early
Don't assume that your deposit is returnable, even if it is described as a 'reservation' deposit. In most countries paying a deposit commits you to the purchase, so don't hand over any money – even to a third party – unless you are sure you want to buy.

6. Choosing on the basis of price
It may be tempting to buy a property for the price of a second hand car, but perhaps the reason it's so cheap is that nobody else wants it.

7. Ignoring the ongoing costs
Even if you hardly use it, keeping an overseas property ticking over costs money. Insurance, maintenance, property management fees, service charges and taxes all add up, so work all this out in advance.

8. Relying on budget airlines
Cheap flights have opened up huge tracts of Europe to property hunters, but don't assume they will always be there. Ask yourself what would happen to your tourist rentals if routes to the little local airport disappeared.

9. Doing things on the cheap
If you want to avoid creating a white elephant, don't cut corners when renovating. If you can't afford the architects, surveyors and craftspeople to bring out your property's potential, look for a different one.

10. Forgetting your heirs
If you want control over how your property is dealt with on your death – and avoid the restrictive inheritance rules in many foreign countries – you need to make a will. You may even need to make two: one here and one there.

Deciding to buy

Buying property abroad is a big decision. For some it is the realisation of a long-held dream – a chance to move somewhere completely different and embrace a whole new way of life. For others it is a hard-headed investment decision. Take the time to think before you leap.

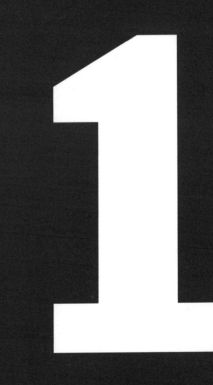

Buying abroad

Buying overseas property successfully is about more than just spotting a bargain and picking your way through what can be a bureaucratic minefield – it involves laying the foundations for what could be one of the biggest financial and emotional investments you ever make.

KEY POINTS

Before you go anywhere near an estate agent, you need to focus on developing:

- clarity about why you want to buy;
- a good grasp of what owning a property in another country genuinely entails; and
- a realistic estimate of what you could afford and how you would finance the investment.

None of these elements is likely to come into your head automatically, but the absence of any of them has the potential to make a mess of the whole exercise – so it pays to do plenty of homework first.

WHY BUY ABROAD?

There are all sorts of reasons why you might consider buying abroad, as shown in the box on the opposite page. Broadly speaking, these can be broken down into three driving motives.

Firstly, you might dream of owning a **holiday home**; secondly, you may have always fancied **moving to sunnier climes**, either relatively early

on in life or later on – perhaps after retirement – as a base in which to while away your autumn years; thirdly, you might consider overseas property to be **a good investment**.

It is possible that all three of these motives underpin your interest in overseas property to a greater or lesser extent. Whatever your reasons, being clear about why you want to buy abroad before you go any further is important because otherwise you could end up choosing a property that does not really meet your needs.

The best property for investment purposes might actually be the kind of place you would never consider living in yourself, for example; similarly a property that would work for you personally as a holiday home might not be appealing to the majority of other tourists.

Therefore, your first goal in deciding whether to buy abroad should be to work out which of these motives is driving you, so that you can think long and hard about the pros and cons of going down the route you are considering and tailor your property search accordingly.

10 reasons to consider buying abroad

1 You enjoy the culture of a particular country or region and would like to explore it in more depth.

2 You have a hobby that you could pursue more enjoyably if you had a base in a different climate, such as golf, skiing or sailing.

3 You have a large family and would like a base for all of you in which to enjoy holidays, together or apart.

4 You have young children and would like to have a base for seaside holidays.

5 You are thinking about ways to boost your retirement finances and think property has good long-term potential.

6 You would like to work and live in a different country.

7 You would like to retire to somewhere with a warmer climate.

8 You have a lump sum to invest and think putting it in property could be a safe option and produce regular income.

9 You have heard about huge potential for capital growth in some areas and would like a slice of the action.

10 You think you would enjoy the challenge of property developing overseas.

SOMEWHERE FOR HOLIDAYS

It is easy to see the appeal of owning a holiday home overseas. The idea of having a place to call your own, which would enable you to experience a different culture at close hand, giving you access to a warmer climate and a more laid-back lifestyle – and which is available to you whenever you want to use it – is very attractive.

You may be interested in a 'classic' villa on one of the Spanish costas, a ski chalet in the Alps or a chic

❝The idea of having a place to call your own overseas, in a warmer climate and with a laid-back lifestyle, is very attractive.❞

apartment in a smart tourist trap. But no matter what kind of property and where it is located, remember that a second home is an expensive thing to own, if only in the sense that the money you are spending on it cannot, therefore, be spent on something else.

Even if you are lucky enough to have the money to support a holiday home without generating letting income from it, it would bring with it a host of bills to pay – from utilities and insurance to paying for someone

to collect the rubbish. Assuming you kept it that long, your heirs could be liable for inheritance tax on the asset.

If you would need your holiday home to earn its keep, you have the extra worry of making sure enough people want to stay in it, at the right time and at the right price; and of being sure the property and its contents are managed and maintained to a standard your clients would expect.

Cheaper options

If money is tight and you are looking to buy a holiday home to use for part of the year but no more, you may consider a timeshare or fractional ownership. In this scenario, you buy a share of a property rather than the full freehold.

Timeshares

The first thing to understand about timeshare is that it is not a way of owning property. What it gives you is guaranteed access to a holiday home for a fixed amount of time each year, generally speaking for a period of 50 or 80 years. The rest of the time the property is used by other timeshare owners.

It is not possible to take out a mortgage on a timeshare, because there is no property for the lender to repossess if you default on the loan –

 For more information and advice on timeshares, contact Euroconsumer, which offers help for consumers buying goods and services across national boundaries within the EU, via www.euroconsumer.org.uk

Timeshares and fractional ownership

Most property experts advise against timeshares, saying they are just an expensive way of paying for an annual holiday, but they may suit you if your heart is set on 'owning' somewhere abroad but you are on a tight budget.

although timeshare companies will normally offer loans if you do not have cash upfront. Shop around if you are thinking about taking up this option.

The legalities of timeshares vary according to where you are buying. Additionally, because timeshare developers tend to like to organise everything from the building of the resort to setting up finance options, it is vital to make sure that you understand and are happy with every aspect of the deal before agreeing to anything. Otherwise, there is a danger of being swept along by a purchase process that can seem to develop its own momentum.

Remember, in a timeshare development every villa or apartment needs to be sold roughly fifty times – once for every week it can be used – in order to hit a sales target. So it is hardly surprising that sales people are keen to get things moving and complete the sale as quickly as possible.

Since the mis-selling scandals of the 1980s, timeshare legislation has been tightened up somewhat, and several major hotel and travel companies operate schemes. But there are still crooks out there, so watch out.

The big advantage of recent legislation in the EU and US is that you now have a minimum ten-day cooling-off period to reflect on what might have felt like a good idea when the timeshare representative was wining and dining you. However, this period of grace only applies if you are buying direct from the timeshare company – resales are not covered, and neither are timeshares involving accommodation on boats.

If you are not offered a cooling-off period in writing, walk away, and if you are looking for a timeshare in Europe, go for companies which are part of the Organisation for Timeshare in Europe (www.ote-info.com), which has a voluntary ethical code to protect timeshare consumers' rights, on top of the legislation.

Fractional ownership

This model, which is already fairly well established in the US, typically involves buying a quarter or a twelfth of a holiday home, for a proportion of its value. The freehold is owned by a specially formed company, in which the purchaser owns the relevant proportion of the shares.

Developers in Europe are beginning to market fractional ownership

13

properties, operating rolling timetables whereby each shareholder is allocated the relevant number of weeks' use per year, and villas and apartments incorporate designated lockers in which to store personal effects for the rest of the time.

Arranging a 'do it yourself' version is another option. Say you have three siblings, for example, and you all want to buy a holiday home together. The four of you might each be able to raise £50,000 to put down, giving you access to a £200,000 property for the equivalent of three months a year each.

" Always take legal advice before you sign any purchase contracts and think carefully about who gets to use the property and when. "

If you opt for any kind of fractional ownership arrangement – even if it involves only friends or family – take legal advice before you sign any purchase contracts. You need to reflect carefully on who owns the freehold, how the shares scheme works and what happens if people want to pull out of the purchase; it is also wise to think carefully about who gets to use the property and when. Raising finance can be a particular issue with such arrangements, since mortgage lenders are unlikely to want to lend against a property in which they can only repossess a share of it if things go badly wrong.

SOMEWHERE TO LIVE

While most people seek a holiday home, for some the decision to buy abroad is part of a wholesale relocation. This calls for considerable research and advance planning.

Working abroad

Apart from a lucky few whose finances enable a more carefree existence, the idea of moving abroad is, for most people, tied up with the ability to find work in the location in question. As such, the decision of whether or not to emigrate is likely to be as much about whether you are able or want to pursue a particular line of work, and about whether you and your family want to uproot yourselves from the UK, as it is about property ownership.

It is almost certainly advisable to rent a property for a while before you commit to buying. This will give you the freedom to think twice about emigrating – or living in a particular location – before you commit yourself to something as life-changing as selling up and moving overseas. Doing so also gives you the time to find the kind of property you would like to live in permanently. After all, this may be a very different kind of place from one in which you would be happy to spend occasional holidays, both in terms of location and the standard of its facilities.

Retiring abroad

Choosing the right area may take on even greater importance if you are thinking about retiring abroad. For some people, the idea of a great retirement is pottering around the garden, looking after the grandchildren, and a few rounds of bridge. For others, moving abroad offers the prospect of a healthier climate, a lower cost of living, a more relaxed pace of life and access to an exciting new culture – indeed some forecasters have predicted that by 2020 one in five British over-55s could be living abroad.

People's reasons for retiring to different areas vary considerably. A study on retirement migration to the Mediterranean found that 48% of British expatriates cited climate as the main reason they had migrated to the Costa del Sol, for example; whereas only 15% of those who had retired to Tuscany put climate at the top of their list of reasons, with childhood or family links, business connections and admiration of Italy itself much more likely to bring about such a move.

Making sure your pensions are sufficient to keep you in the foreign lifestyle to which you would like to become accustomed is an obvious first step when considering whether or not retiring abroad is a realistic option.

❝ Some forecasters have predicted that by 2020 one in five British over-55s could be living abroad. ❞

Even if it does not feel like it at the time you retire – and it may not, especially if you retire early or at a point when you are in good health – access to healthcare and other support networks should also be a major factor. As a pensioner living within the European Economic Area, an E121 form entitles you to the same free treatment as your native counterparts, but depending on where you are

Drawing your pension overseas

You can retire anywhere overseas and still receive your UK state pension. If you retire within the European Economic Area or one of around 20 other countries with which we have a social security deal, your pension will receive the usual annual increments. Elsewhere – and this includes popular retirement destinations such as Canada, South Africa and Australia – your pension will be frozen.

Personal and company pensions will generally be paid abroad, but some will only pay into UK banks, so you may have to pay to transfer the money into the local currency – placing your nest egg at the mercy of exchange rate fluctuations. If you plan to go overseas in advance of drawing such pensions, explore with a specialist financial adviser whether it would be better to transfer the fund to a pension scheme in the country in question.

15

> **" Think dispassionately about overseas property and try to view it as an asset like shares in a company. "**

moving to, you may want to take out private health insurance as well – which could eat significantly into your financial resources.

Two homes?

It is important to think carefully about whether to make a 'clean break' and sell your home in the UK. This will depend partly on your own personal preferences, partly on the extent to which you want to stay near your family and friends, and partly on your financial situation. You may decide it would be better to downsize to a smaller property in the UK, which you could use as the equivalent of a holiday home. Perhaps you could keep a property here and let it out, both to give you some rental income and to use as a base if you eventually decide you want to return? Many retirees who are widowed or become ill while living overseas find that their plans change and they decide to return to the UK.

Joint ownership

Depending on your age and circumstances, another option worth considering might be to buy a property jointly with your adult children; their names could even be on the deeds, with you defined as having a life

interest. Care would be needed to avoid incurring gift tax if you went down this route, though, so make sure you appoint a good financial adviser.

See Chapter 6 for information about how to make a success of moving abroad.

SOMEWHERE TO INVEST

One of the biggest areas of growth in the overseas property market in recent years has been in properties bought for investment purposes – the so-called 'fly-to-let' phenomenon.

Depressed stock markets and continuing uncertainty over long term pension provision, combined with alluring TV shows showcasing apparently profitable overseas properties, have convinced many UK homeowners that a second property overseas could be the answer to all their prayers. Even if investment is not your prime motivation for buying abroad, the chances are that long-term capital growth will be somewhere on the list of criteria you use for choosing a property.

Commercial criteria

Just like in the UK, buying as an investment overseas is part art and part science. Whether you are looking for tourist lets or longer term rentals, you need to buy the right kind of property, in the right area, at the right price. You also need to ensure that it has a 'wow' factor and then market it well, in order to stand a good chance of generating a solid income.

Often the kind of properties that perform best as investments are very different from those you would most want to live in yourself – in the UK , for example, some of the most reliable investments are terraced houses aimed at the student market. Dream properties packed with beautiful features and the latest gadgets can actually be the hardest to make money from.

Market research

You will need to do a lot of research to be confident that you are making the most of your capital investment – even more than you would if you were buying in the UK, where you probably already have a good feel for what the market is like, at the very least in the area where you live.

It is unlikely that your knowledge of areas overseas is anywhere near so comprehensive. You may know that house prices in Spain have been heading upwards, for example, but would you know what's happening within a region, such as Catalonia or Valencia, or within a particular location, like Barcelona or Javea? Even within small distances, investment performance can differ enormously.

Property management

Remember that being a landlord in Europe is very different from being one in the UK – partly because of the distances involved, and partly because tenants' expectations can be higher, since longer contracts and greater

Leaseback schemes

If you are unsure about becoming a landlord, an option you might consider is a 'leaseback' scheme, whereby you buy a newly built property and lease it back to the developer, who guarantees you a fixed income per year, plus free use of the property for an agreed number of weeks.

Leaseback schemes exist in many overseas property hotspots, and have been particularly popular in France, where the government offers a VAT rebate worth 19.6% of the purchase price in order to encourage investors to buy in developments that will improve the availability of quality tourist accommodation.

Leaseback deals typically involve a tie-in of nine years, during which time investors are guaranteed a rental income of between 2 and 6% per year, depending on how many weeks' use they themselves want from the flat.

Always make sure your lawyer studies such contracts in great detail, however, because they can prove problematic if the leaseback developer goes bust, or if the agent who manages lettings fails to hit occupancy targets and guaranteed incomes begin to drop. Bear in mind also that an experienced lawyer can achieve the VAT exemption for you in other, perfectly legal ways.

protection against rent hikes are the norm in many countries.

You need to think carefully about how you would manage the logistics of the arrangement. You may be lucky and have friends who can keep an eye on the property for you – although if you are buying the property as a long-term investment, you might need to think about whether that arrangement is sustainable. Alternatively, you might appoint a management company to handle lettings, but such services come at a cost.

However, even more importantly than all of the above, you should first focus on whether investing in overseas property at all is the right investment for your circumstances.

Think dispassionately about overseas property – rather than in the romantic way we tend to when indulging in a gloriously sunny, wine-fuelled week's holiday – and try to view it as an asset in the same way you would treat shares in a company.

Just as with shares, a whole host of external factors – as well as the internal ones over which you may feel you have more control – affect a property's investment performance over the long term; like interest rates, inflation and market sentiment, to name but a few. Knowing when to sell is also key to success.

Because houses and apartments are expensive things to buy, investing in one in the hope of generating regular income and long-term capital growth means putting an awful lot of eggs in one basket.

Weighing up the pros and cons

If you are having problems deciding if investing in overseas property is right for you, try putting your thoughts down on paper, as this often helps to clarify many people's thinking.

Take a blank sheet of A4 and write yourself a clear and direct question at the top of it, such as 'Should I retire abroad?' or 'Do we want a holiday home (in such-and-such a place)?'.

Beneath the heading, draw up a table with three columns, headed: 'Plus', 'Minus', and 'Interesting'. Then using a watch with a second hand, give yourself exactly two minutes to write down, in the column marked 'Plus', all the positive results of your idea.

Take another two minutes to write down all the negative effects under 'Minus'. Then for a further two minutes, jot down anything you can think of that seems 'Interesting' about it.

According to creative thinking guru Edward de Bono, who developed this technique, seeing your thoughts written down in this way should help you move towards a decision.

If you get stuck, you could try assigning a positive or negative score, from zero to ten, to each of the plus and minus points you have written down, and then add up the score to see whether this helps you make a final decision.

As an experiment, why not try doing this exercise both before and after reading the whole of this book?

For example...

Do we want to buy a retirement home on Lake Garda?		
Plus +	Minus −	Interesting
'We love the Italian people and food' 6	'Most of the properties seem to be flats and we'd rather be in a house' 8	'How busy is it in the height of summer?'
'It's really quiet there' 6	'It was cold when we went in October' 3	'What about a place designed especially for English expats?'
'The kids could come and visit' 7	'Not sure our language is good enough to cope with dealing with doctors about Bob's diabetes?' 9	'Maybe there are places with outbuildings the kids could do up, and make it more of a family affair'
'Our Italian classes have been coming on well' 5	'There wouldn't be much for the grandchildren to do' 7	'Bob likes sailing – do they do that on Lake Garda?'
'We could go to the opera in Milan and Verona' 6	'I'd really miss my friends' 8	'How far is it overland to visit John and Sheila in Nice?'
'Flights are cheap' 4	'We wouldn't know anyone' 5	
'Prices seem all right' 5	'Our house in England wouldn't get much in rent' 6	
'It would be fun starting a new life' 5	'We would have to buy a car out there' 2	
Total +44	-48	

...time to think again?

ASSESSING RISK

When people buy shares-based investments, they tend to buy into collective funds, whereby a management firm, operating in a highly regulated market, holds investments in a wide variety of companies on their behalf. One company's poor performance will hopefully be offset by another's success; funds often include a mixture of shares and bonds, to mitigate any problems with either underlying asset.

People tend not to tie up tens or hundreds of thousands of pounds of capital in shares-based investments. They also tend not to borrow money in order to invest in them; and particularly not money secured against their biggest asset of all – the family home.

" Read about other buyers' experiences in books, magazines or on the internet. "

How many people do you know who would remortgage their house in order to invest in a single company? Not many, unless it was their own company – and yet that is precisely what thousands of British investors are doing when they buy a place in the sun. Accept the scale of the venture you are getting into and do your homework well, and with luck you will make a go of buying an investment property overseas. Close your eyes to the level of commitment required and there is a strong chance you could come a cropper.

INVESTING TIME

Whatever your motivation in buying overseas, you need to think long and hard about the work involved in buying and maintaining such a property. This is not an investment in the same sense that buying an ISA is, where you put some money aside each month and that's it. For most people buying abroad is a life-changing event, so it is important to think realistically about whether you have the time to make a good job of it, before jumping in at the deep end.

INITIAL PREPARATIONS

Before you do anything else, take some time to focus on if and how you might afford to buy a property. You need to set what you think is a realistic budget and, if you would need to borrow to finance that budget, talk to mortgage lenders to see if they would lend you the money.

If possible, spend time talking to people who have already bought overseas, and read about other buyers' experiences in books, magazines or on the internet – there are plenty of web forums out there in which expatriates and people buying abroad share their joys and sorrows. In Chapter 8 there are some suggestions of sources you may find useful.

The more you get to know areas before you start seriously looking at properties, the better. If you have never visited an area, read plenty of guide books and try to get a feel for it from relevant websites before even beginning to consider it as a possible investment location. Never rely solely on your own instincts.

Visit a few areas you might be interested in for holidays, or at least a few long weekends, and rent an apartment there rather than staying in a hotel – to get a better idea of what real homes are like.

Even if you think you know where you want to buy, set aside some time to hunt around overseas estate agents' websites, which can be a good way of finding out what kind of properties are available, and at what price, in different countries and regions. Speak to some 'property finder' agents, who could take on the legwork of finding properties that meet your criteria, albeit for a fee.

Talk to local estate agents, to get a feel for whether other British people have already bought there and how 'geared up' the area is for overseas buyers; and perhaps arrange some exploratory viewings.

Speaking the language can really help minimize the chances of your overseas property dream turning into a nightmare. You may never be fluent, but six months of evening classes combined with some home study, perhaps using audio tapes, CDs or a software package, can help you get to the stage where you can understand the gist of what other people are saying, and can make

yourself understood. This not only makes life easier when you are researching possible locations to buy in, but helps show the locals, and the professionals you will need to work with, that you mean business.

BEFORE YOU SIGN

Once you have narrowed your search, you will then need to take time to find a good lawyer, both in the UK and where you might buy. It is best to talk to your UK lawyer well in advance of buying, so that they can advise you on UK tax and ownership issues and offer guidance on how the local lawyer should handle the purchase.

Allow time to get the money for the deposit and fees together. Check out estate agents' fees and credentials in advance, and give them a clear picture

❝It is best to talk to your UK lawyer well in advance of buying.❞

of your budget and what kind of properties you are interested in. Set aside a fortnight for viewings if possible; arrange to see properties with a few agents, but always be prepared to walk away and try again at a later date or in a different area if nothing suits.

To find a lawyer who specialises in overseas property work, contact the Law Society (www.lawsociety.org.uk allows you to search for English-qualified lawyers who do work overseas). See also page 77.

If you see something that interests you, you will need to line up a surveyor and any other professionals you might want to employ, such as currency brokers, builders or architects. If you are likely to need a translator, look for one as soon as possible, and make sure they will be around throughout this whole process.

Once you have found a property you want to buy, instruct your local lawyer, taking into account your UK lawyer's advice. One of the most vital things to remember when looking for overseas property is that in most countries apart from England, offers are binding – so you cannot make speculative offers on several properties and, on the basis of the sellers' responses, decide which to go for. From the moment you say officially that you want a property, that is taken to be a binding commitment.

Assuming you are sure you want to go ahead, allow yourself time to check all the paperwork thoroughly, making sure your lawyer inserts enough get-out clauses in the initial contract, and that deposits are handled in the correct manner.

In the two or three month period between seeing a property you want to buy and signing the final deed, you will need to be as available as possible to check paperwork, ask and answer questions, deal with mortgage lenders, brokers and the like; and sign papers. If at all possible it helps to be 'on location', but at the very least, make sure you have the time to deal with phone calls, emails and correspondence, and get out there to sign the deed on the appointed day.

Depending on where it is and its state of repair, setting the property up with gas, electricity and telephone connections may take longer than you think, and it is important to sort out insurance straight away.

For more information on how to find and deal with lawyers and how best to handle the buying process, see Chapters 4 and 7.

AFTER YOU SIGN

Once you have signed the final deed, your work as an overseas property buyer is done – but as an owner you will almost certainly need to devote a lot of time and energy to your new purchase.

If you are restoring, rebuilding or refurbishing the property, be prepared for this to eat up your time and energy, even if you have a project manager on site and are overseeing the project from the UK. And if you are letting the property out for income, be prepared for plenty of ongoing effort, both in terms of

---

❗ Preliminary contracts

In France, Spain, Italy and Portugal contracts are signed at a much earlier stage than in Britain. See Chapters 4 and 8 for further details.

Essential tasks

If you are planning on buying a property abroad, there are a range of factors that you should take into account before you proceed.

Initial preparations (6 months)	Before you sign (4-6 months)	After you sign (ongoing until you sell)
Work out budget	Find a translator	Restoration/ refurbishment
Talk to lenders	Find lawyers	
		Appoint and monitor
Get a feel for possible areas/locations	Sort out cash for deposits, fees and other upfront costs	managing agents – oversee maintenance and marketing
Exploratory visits	Find estate agents and arrange viewings	Tax returns
Learn the language	Find surveyors, builders etc Make official offer	Insurance renewals
	Be 'on hand' during buying process and attend signing	
	Set up/transfer utilities Set up insurances	

marketing the property and maintaining it.

This is particularly true if you are letting the property out to tourists; you will need to keep a close eye on the property's performance from the start, including monitoring what the management agency is doing, if you have one; and developing your own marketing plans. Even relatively simple matters such as transferring money between overseas and UK banks can be surprisingly time-consuming, so make allowances.

As time goes on and repeat business builds up, you may be able to take a less hands-on approach to all this, but even if your property turns in a healthy profit and all goes smoothly, you would do well to undertake reviews of your investment at least once a year; and remember to factor in time to deal with tax returns and such like.

CAN YOU HANDLE THE RISK?

As with any other form of investment, you need to think about your attitude to risk before you enter into any overseas property transaction.

Your attitude to risk is partly a function of your temperament – some people like to have a sense of security and predictability around their finances,

> **❝ If you need to borrow in order to fund your investment, the risk multiplies enormously. ❞**

while others are happy to live with a degree of uncertainty. It should also be informed by your level of income; the better off you are, the more adventurous you can afford to be with the income you have that is 'surplus' to your everyday needs. Your age is likely to be a factor, because the older you are the more cautious you may want to be with your 'nest egg'; but equally, if you have a young family to support you are probably less likely to risk blowing a fortune on a speculative investment.

SAFE AS HOUSES

Broadly speaking, the safest investments are ones where your original capital is not put at risk, such as building society deposit accounts and mini-cash ISAs, and those for which you are guaranteed a fixed level of return after a set period, like index-linked National Savings products. The problem with such investments is that over the long term their performance is likely to be unspectacular; and they may not even outstrip inflation.

If you want to beat inflation, many financial advisers would suggest a diversified portfolio of shares-based investments like unit trusts, where your money is invested in a range of assets in different markets – perhaps including UK, European and US stocks – and if you want to try something a bit more risky, more exotic products investing in the Far East, Pacific Rim or Emerging Markets.

With any kind of shares-based investment your capital is put at risk, however – as many investors discovered to their cost when the 'dotcom' bubble burst in 2001.

Relatively speaking, property investments involve less risk to your capital because you are buying a tangible asset which, if you buy wisely, will always retain some intrinsic value – hence the oft-quoted phrase 'as safe as houses'.

The value of any property can fall as well as rise, however, so even if you are able to afford to buy a second home outright your investment may not be as risk-free as you might hope.

FINANCING YOUR PURCHASE

If you need to borrow in order to fund your investment, the risk multiplies enormously. If someone suggested you take out a bank loan in order to buy stocks and shares, you probably would not even entertain the idea, but by remortgaging or taking out a second mortgage in order to buy an overseas property you are effectively doing the same, albeit to buy a different kind of asset.

However safe you think bricks and mortar are as an investment, borrowing against your main home to finance an overseas property is not a scenario to enter into lightly, because it puts your UK property at risk of repossession if you cannot keep up the higher level of repayments.

What about if you take out a separate mortgage to finance the overseas property, either through a UK-based broker or direct through a local bank? If you can continue to afford the repayments and if the value of that property heads upward, you will have done well. But what if something goes wrong and as a result you can no longer afford the repayments, for example if you lose your job or become so ill that you are unable to work? You may have to sell – and fast – and depending on what price you can get, lose a chunk of your capital in the process.

People in the UK tend to assume that property prices have an inbuilt tendency to rise, even though in the early 1990s we saw ample evidence that this is not necessarily the case. And if prices overseas happen to be on a downward spiral at the point where you need to sell your property, you may find yourself in a much worse situation than you expect – particularly if you have mortgaged yourself up to the hilt. For more on selling overseas, see Chapter 7.

The cost of borrowing

Let's say you start off with £100,000 in cash. Buy a £100,000 house outright and if its value falls by 2% per year for five years, you have lost £10,000.

Spend the same £100,000 on a £400,000 house, and if the value falls by the same rate then by the end of five years the house will be worth just £360,000, and depending on the rate at which you have been paying off your mortgage during that time, you will almost certainly still have the majority of your £300,000 loan to pay off, leaving you potentially tens of thousands of pounds worse off than when you started.

Remember also that even small interest rate rises can have a big effect on your monthly repayments. If you borrow £100,000 over 25 years at a rate of 5% the monthly repayment would be £591.27; a rate rise of just 1% would bring that figure to £651.88 – which is an increase of 10% on the original repayment level.

HOW MUCH WILL IT COST?

Before you go any further down the road towards buying, you need to think carefully about how much overseas property ownership could cost you, both in terms of upfront and ongoing costs.

BUYER BEWARE

As when buying in the UK, the easiest way of blowing your initial budget is to be seduced by the 'headline' price of a property, which is often hugely lower than the real cost, when you take into account associated expenditure. But the problem does not stop there, especially if you are buying a second home – because even if you are not using a property full-time, there are costs that mount up regardless of how frequently it is occupied.

To help you pin down how much an overseas property might cost you, use some estate agency websites to find the kind of properties you might be interested in and work out some costings, starting with the headline prices, in as much detail as possible.

Throughout the rest of this book you will find information that can help you do realistic 'ballpark' calculations, although do bear in mind that every property is different, so if you get to the point of considering making an offer on a particular property, make sure you work out more precise costings before you commit yourself.

UPFRONT COSTS

In terms of upfront costs, your main expenditure will be the deposit on the property – the size of which can vary

---

Don't be seduced by the headline price

Upfront costs to take into account:
- Cost of deposit(s)
- Property transfer taxes
- Legal and notary fees
- Estate agents' fees
- Land registry fees
- Surveyor's fees
- Fees for other professionals, eg *gestor*, *geometra*, architect
- Costs of property search (DIY or paying someone else)
- Costs of pre-purchase financial advice
- Renovation costs

Ongoing costs to take into account:
- Mortgage repayments
- Local taxes
- Insurance
- Utilities
- Service charges/community fees
- Property management
- Rentals management/advertising
- Banking costs
- Maintenance/redecoration
- Swimming pool/garden maintenance
- Income tax on rentals

considerably according to what kind of property you are buying, and where. But remember all the other transaction costs, including purchase taxes; professional fees – for example for lawyers, notaries, surveyors, architects, a translator if you need one and, depending on the location, your share of estate agents' fees.

Especially if you are looking for a property purely as an investment, it is sensible to add in the costs of visiting possible locations. You may also want to include the cost of language courses taken in preparation for the venture.

ONGOING COSTS

As for ongoing costs, the biggest burden is likely to be the monthly mortgage repayments to fund the property, but other costs can also mount up, including insurance premiums; local taxes; the cost of utilities; service charges if the property is in an apartment or villa complex; general maintenance costs; the costs of maintaining gardens, swimming pools and the like.

If you are planning to renovate the property, it is vital to get a realistic idea of the likely costs of the project before you set your heart on buying it. A property with a headline price equivalent to £20,000 may end up

costing ten times that once you have made the alterations necessary to bring it up to the standards you, or – if you are renting it out – your clientele, require.

The box on the previous page gives an idea of some of the costs you should think about in addition to the headline purchase price; the table gives an example of how one might go about working out the ballpark costs you could face if you are buying a property (with no renovations necessary) to let out to tourists.

By thinking in advance about such costs, you should find it much easier to gauge what kind of property you can afford and, if you are borrowing to fund the purchase, to approach lenders with a much clearer picture of how much you need to borrow.

Being in the fortunate position of having the ability to buy a property outright does not excuse you from such homework. If you were investing in some sort of collective shares-based investment, like a unit trust or open-ended investment company for example, one of the factors you would use to help you decide which product to go for would be the level of fund manager charges. Using the same discipline, you should be clear about the equivalent annual costs of running your overseas property investment.

For more information on estage agents' fees, see page 153. For details on what size of deposit you must pay – and when – see page 98.

Upfront and ongoing costs

SAMPLE COSTS CHECKLIST FOR A TWO-BEDROOM £150,000 PROPERTY ON AN URBANIZATION IN SPAIN

Upfront costs

Deposit (30%)	£45,000
Property transfer taxes (7%)	£10,500
Legal fees (1%)	£1,500
Notary/Land registry fees	£700
Gestor fees	£250
Cost of viewing/signing visits (two stays of a week's duration each, for two people, at £250 per stay per person)	£1,000
GCSE Spanish course	£70
Total upfront costs	**£59,020***

* Note: this total excludes plus valia tax, a sellers' tax which by convention buyers may be expected to pay, unless they have negotiated otherwise. See page 166 under 'Local capital gains tax' and box on page 106 for more details

Ongoing costs per year

Mortgage repayments (assuming remaining 70% of purchase price is financed by remortgaging over 20 years at a rate of 5%)	£8,400 (£700 per month)
Local taxes including equivalent of council tax and refuse tax	£500
Home insurance (building and contents)	£200
Utility bills (standing charges)	£100
Community fees	£400
Property management (key holding, weekly inspections, liaison with insurers, organising of repairs, redecoration etc)	£700
Rentals management (advertising, maintenance of letting records, etc.)*	£400
Total**	**£10,700**

* Note: this excludes commission on lettings, which is likely
to be charged at 15-20%

** Note: this excludes costs of repairs and redecoration

ESTIMATING RENTAL INCOME

Estate agents and rental management companies can often be heard to refer to properties' 'rental yields', particularly in areas where property investment by foreigners is fairly common. What this means is the rent the property might earn, expressed as a percentage of the purchase price.

Rental yields vary enormously between regions, and even within the same town, village or property development; and depend on a huge number of factors. These are some of the most significant:

- Accessibility.
- Facilities within the property, eg air conditioning, lift access, satellite TV.
- External facilities, eg swimming pool, exterior eating area.
- Proximity of shops and other facilities.
- Distance to the sea, mountains and other attractions.
- Condition of the property, furniture and fittings.
- 'Wow' factor, eg whether it is architecturally 'authentic'.
- Effectiveness of advertising.
- Length of time accepting rentals.

Thinking in terms of rental yields can help you crystallise your expectations of how well a property might perform as an income generator – and because they are expressed in percentage terms they provide a handy way of developing comparisons with other types of investment.

However, rental yields are a fairly blunt tool, so if you are faced with a multitude of estate agents throwing such figures around, it is best to take them with a hefty pinch of salt – and remember that a simplistic yield calculation will not take into account the ongoing costs of the property, as outlined above; or income tax, which is payable on all second home rentals (for more details, see Chapter 5).

The best way to work out rough estimates of potential rental incomes is to look at what other owners of comparable properties in the area are charging by way of rent.

In many areas such information will be readily forthcoming from estate agents. If so, hunt around for independent information to reassure

Rental yield

Rental yield is the rent the property might earn, expressed as a percentage of the purchase price.

How to work out a property's yield:
(Yearly rent achievable ÷ Purchase price) × 100 = Yield
Eg Total lettings £8,000 ÷ Purchase price £150,000 × 100 = 5.33%

To work backwards from a quoted yield to calculate the yearly rent achievable:
(Purchase price × Yield) ÷ 100 = Yearly rent achievable
Eg Purchase price £200,000 × 6% ÷ 100 = £12,000

A rough yield scale:
Poor: 0-4% net
Average/good: 4-6% net
Good/very good: 6-10% net
Excellent: 10+% net

yourself that the rental market is not saturated; if not, you may need to ask yourself if this is a good area to be thinking about letting in – unless you have strong reason to believe the market is 'up and coming' (for more details, see page Chapter 2).

If you are thinking about going for a property that you would let out to tourists, focus particularly on where existing owners are pegging rent levels in the peak season, as these would be the most important part of your earnings and are likely to be relatively non-negotiable.

For the rest of the year, even lower rent levels quoted in advertisements may be hard to achieve, so bear in mind that many owners will accept lower rents than those advertised, or settling for unfilled vacancies. Remember also that it can take many years and a lot of expenditure on advertising to build up a successful holiday letting business from scratch.

HAVE YOU GOT THE MONEY?

Arguably the single most important aspect of the whole process is working out whether you can afford to buy abroad in the first place. So before you go any further you need to take a long hard look at your financial situation. You might use a specialist CD-Rom to help you go through your finances, or just do it yourself on paper.

Bear in mind that even if you were to fund a purchase mainly through borrowing, you would need hard cash to pay for the upfront fees for the property. So, first write down in detail what, if any, cash or capital you have.

Next, work out your monthly income and outgoings. This should give you a rough idea of whether you can meet the ongoing costs of such an investment. Even if you hope to offset some of the costs by earning rental income, base your initial calculations solely on your existing income. This will help you to establish how much 'spare' cash you have to contribute towards the costs of the property, and will present you with the 'worst case scenario' of having to pay for it with no rental income coming in.

TAKING STOCK

Once you have a better idea of what money you have coming in and going out, it is sensible to consult an independent financial adviser, who should be able to do a thorough analysis of your finances and point out any potential flaws in your strategy.

 You can find an Independent Financial Adviser (IFA) via IFA Promotions on the internet. Click onto www.unbiased.co.uk

Work out your budget

Your income	£
– Earnings from your job or self-employment (Less tax and other deductions)	
– Pensions from former employer or your own plans	
– State pension	
– Child benefit and tax credits	
– Other state benefits	
– Interest from savings accounts	
– Income from shares, unit trusts, etc.	
– Other income from investments	
– Miscellaneous	
Total	

Your spending	£
– Mortgage, rent, home maintenance	
– Council tax	
– Water, gas, electricity	
– Food and non-alcoholic drinks	
– Alcohol and tobacco	
– Clothing and footwear	
– Household goods	
– Home insurance, telephone, other household services	
– Medicines, toiletries, hairdressing, other personal items	
– Motoring, fares, other travel	
– Going out, holidays, other leisure	
– Life insurance, medical insurance	
– Money set aside for regular savings	
– Loan repayments (other than mortgage)	
– Premiums due for income protection, critical illness cover	
– Miscellaneous	
Total	

FINANCIAL PRIORITIES

Depending on your age and family circumstances, IFAs tend to work on the principle that there are certain priorities you should concentrate on before making any big investment decision. These include:

- **Having a 'rainy day' fund to cover you in case of emergencies** – if at all possible, try to stash away the equivalent of three to six months' pay in a cash ISA or instant access savings account.
- **Protecting your income** – income protection insurance, also known as long-term disability insurance or permanent health insurance, pays you a monthly amount if you are unable to work because of an illness or disability. To make a successful claim, you will need to prove that you are no longer capable of particular tasks required in your line of work, for example driving or seeing a computer screen. Policies pay out until you recover and go back to work, or until you die or reach the policy termination age, which is usually 65. The most you can insure is usually 60% of your gross income. Critical illness insurance pays a lump sum in the event of you being diagnosed with one of a set number of medical conditions, ranging from blindness and kidney failure to stroke, cancer, heart attack and multiple sclerosis. Some policies will also pay out if you are affected by total permanent disability, or are diagnosed with a terminal illness and given less than 12 months to live.
- **Protecting your dependants** in case of death – as a minimum you should have a life policy that would pay the mortgage off if you died, but you may also want to provide for a further lump sum to cover living costs, pay for your children's university education, or fund the costs of childcare. As a general rule, look for policies that pay out at least ten times your salary.
- **Paying for your retirement** – putting away sufficient money to fund your autumn and winter years has always been a vital aspect of financial planning, but never more so than now, with final salary pension schemes fast becoming a thing of the past, and a widening gap between state pension provision and future retirees' income needs. Remember that paying for long term care is also likely to become a bigger issue in the future as life expectancy rises. If you are thinking about investing in an overseas property as part of your plans to fund your retirement, it is essential to take a long, hard look at how owning such a property would stack up against other options, like pension contributions.

If you do not have all these bases covered, your IFA should advise you to think twice about taking on the risk of stretching your finances to support the purchase of an overseas property; income protection should be a particular concern if your plans involve remortgaging on the basis of your income being able to afford two properties.

❝The most important aspect of the whole process is working out whether you can afford to buy in the first place.❞

Questions a financial adviser would ask you

We asked an independent financial adviser to suggest five key questions potential second home buyers should ask themselves when deciding whether or not they can afford to buy overseas.

1. Why do you want the property?
Are you simply trying to 'keep up with the Jones'? Do you want to retire abroad, is it for investment, or a combination of reasons? Have you checked out whether rental markets are saturated? Have you thought realistically about rental potential and how you would market it? Can you really afford to own two properties, even if only temporarily?

2. What finance will you need?
If you are buying outright, great. If not, would you remortgage or take out a loan overseas? Do you have the language to negotiate that? What rate would you get? Where will the deposit come from? What about currency risk? What about maintenance costs? What about capital gains tax and inheritance tax?

3. Are you of working age?
If so, what happens if you lose your job? If not, is your pension guaranteed or linked to with-profits rates - if so what happens if rates are poor? What happens if one of you dies?

4. What happens if airline prices go up?
Could you, and your potential tenants, still afford to go there? What alternative methods of transport are there?

5. What about tax?
You need to consider capital gains tax, income tax on rentals, and inheritance tax - which could affect in whose names you buy the property. What contacts do you have to help you with all this overseas?

SOURCES OF FINANCE

Once you have worked through your finances and produced rough estimates of what an overseas property might cost, and thought about how rental earnings might help it earn its keep, your next step should be to work out how best to borrow the money you would need to fund the purchase.

REMORTGAGING

Remortgaging is likely to be an attractive option if you have built up a substantial chunk of equity in your home and want to take advantage of it. Many people in the UK could save money by renegotiating mortgage deals, so it is well worth finding out how much your premiums would rise if you borrowed the balance of the overseas property purchase price on top of your existing loan.

Talk to a few lenders to see what kind of deals are out there, but remember you may have to pay redemption fees if you are tied in to your current provider. There are valuation, arrangement and legal fees to pay too – which could add up to nearly £1,000 – although a new lender may pick up some of these if you negotiate hard enough.

UK mortgage vs overseas mortgage

Mortgage secured on UK property		Mortgage secured on overseas property	
Pros	Cons	Pros	Cons
May be cheaper if you stay with existing lender	Puts your main home at risk	Less risk to main home	Ongoing currency risk
May negotiate cheaper lending for existing loan into the bargain	Costs – valuation of UK property, legal fees, etc.	Potentially lower interest rates (especially useful if you have the money to buy outright and keep this in high interest-bearing UK account)	Administrative hassle of transferring money each month
No currency risk	May be more expensive than foreign loan	Keeps admin of overseas property separate	Can be difficult to find a lender

The obvious disadvantage of remortgaging, apart from the possible costs, is that it puts your main home at risk if you cannot afford the new, higher level of repayments.

SEPARATE MORTGAGE

The alternative to remortgaging is to take out a separate mortgage, usually secured on the overseas property. You could do this through a foreign lender – or a UK-based broker who specialises in securing mortgages from foreign banks – or apply for a non-sterling mortgage from a UK lender, if such a product is available at a competitive rate. Either way, remember that your repayments would fluctuate not just according to the mortgage rate, but also due to changes in the exchange rate when you transfer your repayment money into the local currency.

Taking this approach can be particularly worthwhile if loan rates in the country you are borrowing in are lower than those in the UK. In fact some IFAs advise that if this is the case, even if you have the cash to buy an overseas property upfront it is worth taking out a local mortgage and keeping the cash in a high interest account in the UK, enabling you to earn more in interest than the loan is costing you abroad. Then if the respective rate positions change, you can pay off the overseas loan in full.

Most lenders, both in the UK and overseas, are conservative when considering applications for second home loans; buy-to-let mortgages are much harder to obtain and are practically unheard-of in continental Europe, for example. As a minimum, lenders will want proof that you can cover all your existing outgoings, plus the proposed extra repayments, from a third of your net income.

CURRENCY RISK

A final issue that it is vital to think about before you go anywhere near making an offer on a property is currency risk. As well as affecting your ongoing costs, if you take out a mortgage in a different currency, even relatively small fluctuations in exchange rates can radically reduce or increase your buying power in the months between searching for properties and money changing hands (see box on page 36).

> **❝ Even relatively small fluctuations in exchange rates can radically alter your buying power. ❞**

There are several ways around this problem, the first being – assuming you think rates are looking favourable – to buy currency early and hold onto it until the point you need to transfer it into the seller's account. This relies on you having a suitable account in which to keep the money, though; and on you having enough cash upfront to buy the currency straight away.

How exchange rate shifts alter your buying power

Where £1 =	What a €100,000 property would cost you
€1.35	£74,074
€1.40	£71,429
€1.45	£68,966
€1.50	£66,667
€1.55	£64,516
€1.60	£62,500

- Firms must give key information in a straightforward manner and not hide it in the fine print.
- Advisers must meet certain training and competency requirements.
- Advisers and intermediaries must disclose information about the commissions they are getting, and whether they deal with the whole market or just one lender.
- Borrowers should receive a summary document showing the key facts of the mortgage in a standardised, comparable, easy-to-understand format to help with shopping around.
- Any complaints which cannot be resolved with the lender may be taken to the Financial Ombudsman Service.

Another option available from currency brokers is to 'forward buy', which means booking your currency in advance, at an agreed exchange rate which is fixed for up to two years. You will normally only need to pay a 10% deposit upfront to exercise this option, which is particularly useful if you are buying 'off plan' and therefore have a long lead-time before needing to pay the bulk of the money.

A third approach is to set up a 'limit order' or 'stop loss' deal with a broker, whereby your currency purchase is triggered if and when the exchange rate reaches an upper or lower level, agreed in advance – although again, you will need the cash upfront in order to pursue this option.

REGULATION OF PROPERTY INVESTMENTS

The Financial Services Authority regulates the mortgage industry in the UK. Its rules say:

Lenders and brokers dealing with 'first charge' loans – that is, main mortgages where the lender has first call on the property and can repossess it if you default – are regulated by the FSA. This includes most firms dealing with 'equity release' loans, which could form part of any remortgage deal you negotiate in order to extend your borrowing.

The FSA has particular concerns about the 'equity release' sector of the mortgage industry, having conducted mystery shopping exercises which revealed sub-standard fact-finding and advice, especially relating to borrowing in order to invest, from a selection of financial advisers.

Because so many factors can affect overseas property investment, malpractice from advisers could in any case be extremely hard to prove, but it is probably fair to say that the FSA's concerns suggest parts of the industry may be offering extra borrowing in a somewhat cavalier fashion, so exercise particular caution.

You can check that any lenders and advisers you deal with are registered with the FSA, and obtain further details on your rights with respect to mortgages and investment advice, by visiting the Consumer information section of the FSA's website, www.fsa.gov.uk.

It is important to stress that FSA rules do not cover 'second charge' mortgages, which offer an alternative way of taking out a further loan secured against your property; so be even more circumspect when considering such deals.

If you take out a mortgage secured on an overseas property, this loan will be covered by whatever regulations exist in the country in question; although under an EU agreement on cross-border 'out of court' disputes you would file any complaint through the FSA – which would then pass it on to the relevant body. For more information on this scheme, called FIN-NET, visit http://europa.eu.int/comm/internal_market/finservices-retail/finnet/index_en.htm.

The Federation of Overseas Property Developers and Agents (www.fopdac.co.uk) has members specialising in overseas property finance, although FOPDAC membership does not confer any additional statutory protection.

ALTERNATIVES TO BUYING ABROAD

Before you go ahead and start looking for that overseas property you have been dreaming about, it is worth taking a little time to consider the alternatives:

- Finding somewhere to rent regularly – a commonly cited reason for buying abroad is that it would be nice to have a place that felt like home, and that one could keep going back to. But why not achieve this by finding a place you could rent on a regular basis, thus retaining the ability to visit frequently but without the added cost and responsibility of ownership?
- Buying with friends and family – especially if money is tight, or if you are not sure you would use an overseas property enough to justify the outlay, why not think about a

 For UK mortgage advice see 'Consumer Information' on the Financial Services Authority (FSA) website at www.fsa.gov.uk
Alternatively, call the FSA Customer Helpline 0845 606 1234

joint purchase with friends or family? (see warning box on page 14).

- Buying in the UK – a buy-to-let investment in the UK may not seem as glamorous as one overseas, but it may be just as profitable; even if you are looking for a holiday home, you may find that one in the UK meets most of your needs and is cheaper, once distance and convenience are taken into account. Again, fractional ownership is an option.
- Investing in a property fund – if investment is your prime motivation, why not consider investing in a property-based investment fund, whereby your money is pooled with that of other investors and invested in a portfolio of properties, normally grouped by geographical location (for example an Eastern Europe, Baltic or Balkan fund)?
- Investing in land – again, if profit is your prime reason for buying abroad, you could think about buying some land rather than a pile of bricks and mortar; it is likely to be cheaper and, especially if you buy wisely and add value by securing planning permission for future development, you could do well. In some cases people have turned in a tidy profit by purchasing land plots in sought-after locations and selling them on a few years later.

Residential property funds

Although collective investment schemes that invest in commercial property such as shops and offices have been available to UK investors for some time, it is only fairly recently that residential-based funds – already popular in the US and some other countries – have emerged in the UK.

Investors buy shares in a fund that then invests in residential property, normally within a defined geographical region. Depending on the fund's performance the investors receive dividends according to a strictly defined schedule, and after a set period the fund is either liquidated and the proceeds split according to the initial agreement; or investors are able to sell their shares and receive a portion of the growth.

Before government legislation to establish real estate investment trusts (REITs) in the UK, some collective residential property investment vehicles aimed themselves deliberately at speculative investors, for example by investing in relatively high risk property in Eastern Europe.

If you want to invest in any kind of collective investment product, get it checked carefully by a qualified lawyer and/or financial adviser before making a decision.

Location, location

Where you decide to invest will be influenced by why you want to buy abroad in the first place. Some people already have a particular location in mind. Others are less decided and will need to weigh up factors such as climate, accessibility and ease of letting in their calculations.

Where to buy?

Once you have decided you are serious about buying overseas, you need to think carefully about what sort of location might meet your needs. You may already have a particular place in mind, but it makes sense to consider all the factors likely to affect your enjoyment of a property there.

If you are buying purely or even partly as an investment, you may need to think more carefully and decide between several locations, in order to maximise your chances of the property being a money-spinner.

Whatever your motive for buying abroad, these are some of the main points to consider when choosing where to buy.

CLIMATE

It is no coincidence that people from the UK and other northern European countries are the keenest of overseas property buyers. Colder, wetter climates and shorter winter days are enough to make even the most patriotic of Britons dream of year-round access to sunnier shores.

Make sure you research climates carefully though, rather than relying on a couple of weeks in July or August as a benchmark; and if you are looking for somewhere you might use yourself, think realistically about when in the year you could be free to visit, and what sort of climate you would like when you go.

This is particularly important if you need the property to generate income; in most of Europe the peak letting season is in the summer, which means you will need the property to be let out at that point – leaving you free to use the property only in the potentially much colder and wetter low season.

SURROUNDINGS

No matter where you are thinking of buying, think carefully about the physical surroundings, and not just how exotic or attractive the area feels on a sunny July afternoon. Focus on

Take a rain check

To find out about weather across Europe, check out relevant tourist guide books and websites, or visit the Met Office website, www.metoffice.gov.uk, which provides five day forecasts for 66 cities along with year-round climate descriptions for a variety of European countries and regions. Its Weathercall service covers more than 200 European cities and resorts, and can be accessed via a premium rate telephone number or SMS text messaging service. For further details of subscription packages, contact 0871 200 3985.

the extent to which it meets your clearly defined needs.

If you are buying a holiday home purely for yourselves, reflect on the kind of environment that is your ideal. Are you the kind of people who like to explore hills and forests, traipse around museums and galleries, or laze around on the beach? If you have children or may be visited by grandchildren, is there enough to keep them occupied?

If you are likely to want the property to generate letting income, consider how attractive the location is to other people as well as to yourselves. You may find a particular town in mid-France an ideal place for a holiday home because you have family there, for example, but other people might find the place unremarkable.

Living somewhere permanently or even temporarily is very different from staying there for a week or two in the summer, so if the property is going to serve as a full time home for any length of time – or if you are going to let it out to tenants all year round – check out all the local amenities.

How close is the nearest supermarket, for example? What about the nearest doctor's surgery, pharmacy, school, garage, computer supplies shop, swimming pool maintenance firm and whatever else is important to keep modern life running as normal?

ACCESSIBILITY

For most people buying abroad, it is important for their property to be accessible, and this is doubly so if you are looking to generate income from lettings.

This does not mean you have to buy within a two-minute radius of an

Urban vs. rural

Some people's rural idyll might be unbearably remote for others. Think about facilities and transport before you buy

Urban		Rural	
Pros	Cons	Pros	Cons
More attractive to long-term renters	May be less attractive to tourists	May be more attractive to tourists	Fewer amenities
Closer to amenities	Could be noisier, more traffic etc	More secluded	Less accessible
More accessible	May have less community spirit	Community may be more close-knit	Less attractive to long-term renters

41

Can you get there?

Think about how you and your possible clients would get there if the airline closed the route. Is the area accessible by train, boat or car, and at what cost?

airport, but the travel industry works on the assumption that, as a rule of thumb, a quarter of potential visitors will be put off if they have to travel for more than an hour from the airport at the end of their journey. If the travelling time rises to 90 minutes, half will not bother.

Clearly there will be exceptions to this rule – we would all consider a longer drive if we thought there was something really unusual at the end of it – but if your property is fundamentally nothing special, think long and hard about how distance might affect its earning potential.

It may well be that the only way you can afford the kind of property you want is to look deeper into the wilds of the countryside; or that the particular house you have chosen is thousands of metres up a mountain, and that is the way you like it; in which case, make sure you are happy

that the inconvenience is, for you, a price worth paying. Do not assume everyone will think in the same way, though, and remember that this may be important if and when you come to sell the property.

FLIGHT TIMES

On a more general note, remember that however attractively priced budget airlines can be, and however much they have opened up new areas for holidaymakers and potential homebuyers, they are not all suddenly flying supersonic.

If you add together check-in and baggage collection times, flight times and travel at either end, what seems like a short journey can pretty soon start to feel like an odyssey – and that is without even thinking about any delays that might occur along the way. So if this is meant to be your bolt-hole, be realistic about how much time you would really spend in the place.

Remember also that airlines have their own priorities, and these may not always coincide with yours. Especially if you are thinking about buying an area newly opened up by a budget route, think about how you and your possible clients would get there if the airline closed the route. Is the area accessible by train, boat or car, and at what cost?

Budget airlines have expanded dramatically in recent years, but you need to keep up to date with routes and fares. A website such as www.skyskanner.net will give you the latest details.

CULTURAL ISSUES

The effects of a different language, history and culture on your enjoyment of an overseas property can hardly be under-estimated – both in terms of the ease or otherwise of the buying process and, if you are buying for personal use, of your ability to deal with everyday life and 'fit in' with the locals afterwards.

Many people enter into the process of buying overseas with the attitude that legal and administrative systems in other countries are either unnecessarily bureaucratic or frustratingly laissez-faire; or sometimes both. Systems and customs do differ between countries, but the truth is that engaging in financial transactions with strangers and dealing with 'the authorities' anywhere can be a complex and time consuming affair.

Just like in the UK, picking your way through the minefield successfully requires both a good understanding of how the system works and the ability to apply pressure to the relevant agencies where appropriate.

For every British overseas property owner who describes their buying process as a nightmare, another reports that everything went surprisingly smoothly, adding that learning about how things are done differently in other countries rather than focusing on local 'inefficiencies' can enrich your buying experience enormously.

If you are interested in buying in a market that has relatively recently opened up to overseas buyers, establishing clear title to the property can be much more complicated than is usually the case when buying in the UK. This is because of differences in the way properties are handed down from generation to generation;

> **❝For every British overseas property owner who describes the buying process as a nightmare, another reports that everything went surprisingly smoothly.❞**

disparate claims on properties in previously war-torn areas; and in some countries, the relatively new nature of western-style Land Registry systems.

For ideas about useful sources of information in various countries, see Chapter 8.

Case Study Following the local customs

David and Wendy Scott bought a house in the Limousin region of France after two decades of holidaying in the same area. Mr Scott speaks fondly of an unexpected custom the couple encountered after completing the purchase of the house: 'After signing the papers we went to our new house and the previous owner insisted on us going round and marking out the boundary together, by halving bricks and burying them under the soil. This is the locals' way of marking out their respective territories in a way that helps minimise future disputes.'

Researching different areas

Before you plunge headlong into searching for properties you might be interested in, it makes sense to arm yourself with background information about a range of different areas, perhaps in different countries, that might contain properties with the potential to meet your needs.

Chances are you already know something about parts of one or a number of overseas countries, having visited for business or pleasure. But do you know enough to make an informed decision that the places you have seen and been impressed by are the 'best in class' in terms of achieving what you want to achieve through owning overseas?

Choices about where to buy, like choices about where to go on holiday, are driven largely by personal taste. But that does not preclude you from being thorough when deciding if and where to buy, and thinking imaginatively about options that might not be immediately apparent.

If what you want is a holiday home close to the sea with year-round sunshine, and you are prepared to look a bit further afield, for example, why not find out about the Canary Islands, Dubai or even Cape Verde,

rather than assuming that the Costa del Sol is the place to look?

Particularly if you are trying to find out about areas outside the European Union, discovering even the most basic information that might affect your experience of buying or owning property can be a struggle – but your perseverance will be well-rewarded if the end result is a purchase that fulfils, and perhaps exceeds, your expectations over the long term.

GENERAL INFORMATION SOURCES

For general information about different countries across the world, a good place to start is the UK Foreign Office, whose website includes detailed profiles on more than 200 countries, from Afghanistan to Zimbabwe; covering everything from geography and recent political developments to information about the economy, health and human rights records. The site also gives details

 A useful source of information is the UK Foreign Office, whose website at www.fco.gov.uk includes detailed profiles on more than 200 countries.

about the UK's diplomatic representation in the country, and in most cases there are links to official government websites.

For further general information, it is well worth looking at official embassy websites, and for marketing information about possible areas worth looking in, national and local tourist authority sites can be useful, so long as you take their purple prose with a pinch of salt.

INFORMATION ABOUT PROPERTY MARKETS

One of the problems intrinsic to buying overseas property is the lack of reliable, independent information about property markets at a national and sub-national level.

In the UK property data such as the Halifax and Nationwide house prices indices, Hometrack surveys and the Royal Institution of Chartered Surveyors' lettings market survey, are frequently reported in the national press, offering up-to-date information about trends in

prices and other aspects of property investment at a national, regional and even postcode level. Such data is much more difficult to come by for other countries, making it extremely difficult to gain anything more than a cursory sense of how residential property markets are performing.

"Specialist magazines and websites can help you keep up to date with latest developments."

Overseas property coverage in the national press and specialist magazines and websites can help you keep up to date with the latest developments, and it can be worth visiting overseas property exhibitions to get a flavour of the kinds of places you could buy in – although bear in mind that these almost exclusively cover new-build developments.

Don't rush into things

Once you have decided you are interested in buying an overseas property, especially a holiday home, there is a strong temptation to rush things. The idea of being able to start holidaying in your own dream home is very appealing, and we in the UK have also been used to property prices heading inexorably upwards, which piles on additional pressure to act fast - especially if you are stretching your finances in order to afford it.

Even if investment is not your prime motivation in buying, it is well worth putting the effort in at the research stage, to ensure you end up with a property that will stand the test of time. You may own this property for the rest of your life and possibly pass it on to your children or other relatives at some stage - in the grand scheme of things, what difference does it make if its purchase is delayed by a few months while you hone your decision making?

45

Get the facts

Always ask agents where their information comes from and if possible, verify their data with the original sources.

The most dependable source for country-by-country analyses is almost certainly the annual Royal Institution of Chartered Surveyors' European housing market survey, which looks in depth at what is happening in the property markets of 17 European countries.

This is a good starting point if you are setting out to develop a broad understanding of different countries' relationships with bricks and mortar in the most obvious European countries, like France, Spain and Italy. The organisation does also produce a global survey, but this focuses on cities rather than entire national markets. For further information, visit the RICS website at www.rics.org.uk.

Estate agents and developers will often fire statistics about property market trends at you, and at any given time, there will be no shortage of property 'hotspots' being talked about. Sometimes – although by no means always – genuine evidence will lie

behind such predictions; always ask agents where their information comes from and if possible, verify their data with the original sources. Remember also that, as with shares-based investments, past performance is no guarantee of what will happen in the future.

FINANCIAL INFORMATION

There are a variety of sources for macro-economic statistics to help you build up a picture of different countries' wider economies. This kind of information can be vitally important when making long-term investment decisions, and is unlikely to be made readily available to you by estate agents whose vested interest is in you making a purchase, rather than a sensible financial decision.

The Organisation for Economic Development and Cooperation produces a host of statistics on everything from environmental issues to health, education and taxation in its member countries, at www.oecd.org. In terms of economic data, figures on consumer prices indices, unemployment rates, hourly earnings and exchange rates are available. Reading magazines like *The Economist* and *Money Week* can help you develop an overview of global, regional and national economic trends.

 The European Central Bank publishes information about interest rates offered by banks and other financial institutions in EU countries on its website, www.ecb.int

Loans

Availability of local mortgages, and the terms of such loans, may be an issue for you; to find contact details for lending institutions in different countries, you could start with the banking section of US-based website www.escapeartist.com, which publicises a wide variety of information sources of relevance to people thinking about moving abroad. Another list of overseas banks appears on the www.qualisteam.com website.

Taxation

The Inland Revenue produces tax advice for people considering a move abroad, or buying a property that might produce income liable for taxation. The Centre for Non-Residents deals with non-resident individuals, non-resident trusts, and certain non-resident companies; it also operates and provides advice on all aspects of the Non-Resident Landlords Scheme; handles claims and applications for relief by all categories of non-residents under double taxation treaties; considers individual entitlement to UK personal allowances, and provides guidance on the residence and domicile status of individuals. It also provides guidance about UK National Insurance liabilities whilst abroad and on EC Regulations and bi-lateral convention rules on Social Security. It also deals with the tax implications of transfers of assets abroad.

Tax and benefits

Tax

If you buy in a country which has a double taxation treaty with the UK, you should not be taxed twice for income tax on rentals and capital gains tax. To find out more about your likely liabilities, ask your local tax office for the following leaflets:

IR20 – Residents and non-residents. Liability to tax in the UK

IR138 – Living or retiring abroad? A guide to UK tax on your UK income and pension

IR139 – Income from abroad? Guide to UK tax on overseas income

IR140 – Non-resident landlords, their agents and tenants

Benefits

The Department for Work and Pensions provides information about entitlement to state benefits while overseas, and the Pension Service (part of the DWP) provides more detailed information about retiring abroad. For further information and to find local contact details to discuss matters further, follow the links on the DWP website from www.dwp.gov.uk/lifeevent/benefits/index.asp and www.thepensionservice.gov.uk.

To contact the Centre for Non-Residents, telephone 0151 472 6192/6137, visit www.inlandrevenue.gov.uk/cnr/index.htm

Narrowing your search

Once you have considered areas that might be worth exploring, and have done some initial research to find out about property buying there, the next step is to identify some specific locations that interest you, and arrange some visits.

You may at this point also want to do some initial homework to identify lawyers and other professionals, like estate agents and property finding agents, whose services might prove useful if you decide to go ahead.

" Visit at two contrasting times of year to find out what the area is like at its busiest and quietest. "

If at all possible, set aside time for week or fortnight-long visits, to give you a chance to ponder the area in a relaxed manner, rather than rushing around like a headless chicken. Try to visit at two contrasting times of year, so as to get a feel for what the area is like when at its busiest and quietest.

Avoid the temptation to go on organised 'inspection trips' run by estate agents and developers, which are usually brief and superficial, and are often little more than 'hard sell' sessions (see page 70).

Rather than booking into a hotel, book and stay in a house or flat. If nothing else, this will give you an idea of how easy or difficult it is to find accommodation in the area and how much it costs to rent as a tourist. It may also give you a valuable insight into what kind of facilities are on offer from your potential competitors, and if you get to meet or speak directly to the owners you may even be able to 'pick their brains' about what life as a second home owner in that area is like.

No matter where in the world you visit with a view to deciding whether it would suit your purposes as an overseas property owner, there are a whole host of factors to assess while you are there.

ASSESSING POTENTIAL LOCATIONS

Depending on your purpose in buying abroad, and whether or not you are looking to generate income from a property, the relative importance of the factors shown in the diagram opposite will vary.

The level of tourist development in an area is likely to be important to you if you are planning to buy a holiday home, for example, and especially if you would want it to earn its keep from lettings income – partly

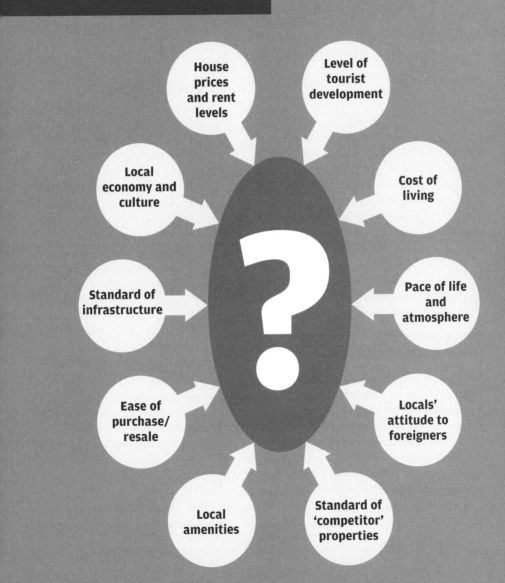

FACTORS TO CONSIDER WHEN ASSESSING POTENTIAL LOCATIONS

The importance you attach to various factors depends on your main reason for buying property abroad. In considering each one you need to think how they could be significant.

House prices and rent levels

Level of tourist development

Local economy and culture

Cost of living

Standard of infrastructure

?

Pace of life and atmosphere

Ease of purchase/ resale

Locals' attitude to foreigners

Local amenities

Standard of 'competitor' properties

because you may want to take advantage of tourist attractions yourself, and also because if an area attracts large number of tourists, a potential rental market probably already exists.

> **❝ The standard of infrastructure, and the amenities available locally, are likely to be important whatever your reason for buying. ❞**

Factors like the standard of infrastructure, and the amenities available locally, are likely to be important whatever your reason for buying, and could take on particular significance if you are looking for long-term rental contracts. Driving for 20 minutes down a dirt track to find the nearest bakery might seem charming when all you want is a couple of weeks' relaxation, but people looking for a place to call home are more likely

to be attracted to a property where shops, restaurants and a cinema are all within easy striking distance.

Pace of life and atmosphere, and locals' attitude to foreigners, can obviously only be judged subjectively, but such issues can be vital if you are looking to relocate to an area, so it is important to think about them in terms of their likely impact on future buyers, even if you only plan to visit rarely.

RURAL PROPERTIES

Remember also that buying in a rural area, and especially buying a property that needs considerable renovation work, could raise issues you have never previously thought about – which may affect the speed of the buying process, and create additional expense.

If your dream is to buy a property in the middle of nowhere, and especially to renovate a dilapidated building, the buying process could throw up lots of unforeseen problems. For example:

- Gaining planning permission for your proposed changes before you complete the purchase would be essential, so you would need to commission architects' plans and start the application process as soon as you see somewhere you like – and potentially lose the property to another buyer while you wait for the result. Bear in mind that the rules as they currently stand may not even allow the property to be inhabited.
- If you bought a property that is not already connected to essential

---

The right kind of tourism

Just because an area is popular with tourists does not necessarily mean it is a good bet for generating letting income from a holiday home. In many destinations, tourism is dominated by package tours staying in hotels or apartments.

You may be able to negotiate bulk deals for tour operators to fill your accommodation during their peak seasons, but only at relatively low rates. In off-peak periods, visitor numbers may tail off almost completely, and flights may be hard to come by.

---

services like electricity and mains water, the costs of connection would be your responsibility and could be prohibitively high, so you would need advice from a surveyor and/or the relevant utility companies before going any further with the purchase.

- Updates to building regulations mean that old properties that have not been occupied or updated for a long time could need expensive remedial work, including rewiring to meet modern electrical standards. The buying process may throw up specific issues relating to, for example, having to meet new standards for septic tanks. You may also need to commission special surveys on the property, for example to check for asbestos, lead and termite damage.

It is important to make yourself aware of all these issues, investigate them thoroughly and assess the likely implications – in terms of cost and the time it would take to undertake renovations – before deciding to opt for this kind of property.

LOCAL COSTS

Cost of living may be important to you if you are looking for somewhere to live, and especially in retirement. You may be able to form some view of cost of living when visiting, but if you want a more objective view, look out for indices such as those published by Mercer Human Resource Consulting and the Economist Intelligence Unit.

As for house price and rent levels – and the ease or otherwise of resale – try to look dispassionately at how the property market is operating in the area. Does it seem that properties are being marketed mainly, or even exclusively, at foreign investors? If so, might this restrict your market when you come to sell? Can local people afford the levels of rent you would need to charge to cover your costs?

Up-and-coming areas

Up-and-coming areas – generally the best bet if you want medium or long-term capital growth – are the holy grail of many an overseas property investor. They can be tricky to spot, and there is also the danger that this year's emerging market could become next year's white elephant. So what signs of good long-term investment potential should you look out for?

- Look for areas undergoing significant infrastructural improvement, for example where new airports or motorway links are being built. These can cut down journey times and improve accessibility to areas

 Look out for cost of living indices such as those published by Mercer Human Resource Consulting and the Economist Intelligence Unit.

outside the more obvious and expensive 'hotspots'.

- Big international events like the Olympics, World Cup or other sports championships attract investment and can help bring about long-term regeneration, as well as raising an area's profile for tourists – although bear in mind that the long-term benefits of such events can be short-lived and over-hyped.
- If major international companies relocate or expand into an area, this is usually a sign that it is on the way up economically. Such companies can also be a useful source of potential tenants, although remember that firms can disappear just as quickly as they arrive so try to verify that inward investments are part of a wider picture of economic growth.

WHICH KIND OF PROPERTY?

No matter where you are looking, you are likely to face numerous choices along the way. Do you want an apartment or a house, for example? Should it be in a city or large town, or out in the countryside? Should you opt for a new property with a guaranteed rental option, or go it alone and build up your own lettings business?

" This year's emerging market could become next year's white elephant. "

There are pros and cons to each option, and it can be helpful to work through these in advance of organising property viewings – although it is also important to be flexible and not just arrange to see several examples of exactly the same kind of property.

There are no hard-and-fast rules to help make your choice easier, but common sense suggests a few rough guidelines.

Property to let

If you are looking for a holiday home that can generate letting income, apartments and villas in well known tourist regions are probably a good bet. Properties on golfing complexes, those with swimming pools and well-located ski properties have 'added value' and are likely to perform best. Sea views and easy access to a beach can help attract clients. Look for year-round appeal if at all possible. Prices for good properties will be at a premium though, so do not expect this to be a cheap option.

 Some countries, especially those outside the EU, impose restrictions on foreigners' ability to own property and/or land. There are ways of getting round this problem, but these are not always straightforward. To find out more, see page 80.

Location checklist: some of the main factors to consider when comparing locations

Close to airport and/or ferry terminal	✓
Good/improving road and rail links	✓
Well established tourist market	✓
Low unemployment	✓
Low inflation	✓
Low cost of living	✓
Affordable house prices	✓
Good rent levels	✓
Affordable mortgage rates	✓
Evidence of dynamic (upward) housing market, without over-heating	✓
Good health service	✓
Good schools and higher education sector	✓
Close to beach, mountains and other attractions	✓
Double taxation treaty with UK	✓
Evidence of inward investment by international companies	✓
Welcoming attitude to foreigners	✓
Property market accessible to locals as well as foreigners	✓
Close to possible sources of tenants, eg universities, business parks	✓
Close to green space	✓
Interesting history/culture	✓
High level of English-speaking residents	✓
Availability of rental management companies	✓

Top ten issues when assessing rental markets

1. **Demand** – who might be interested in renting your property, and over what period? If you are thinking about renting on long-term contracts rather than just in the holiday season, would you able to appeal to expatriates, locals, or both? Are these markets sustainable?

2. **Rent levels** – what are other owners charging for similar properties? What sorts of facilities and mod cons are considered 'normal' at such prices? Are rents on the way up or down?

3. **Contractual issues** – what legal arrangements are standard between landlords and tenants, and are rent levels pegged or monitored by the state?

4. **Ease of resale** – who might want to buy the property if you came to sell it?

5. **Tax** – what would be your liabilities for capital gains tax when you sold, and for income tax on rentals. How much would ongoing property-based taxes cost?

6. **Letting agents** – how many are there, and how competitive are their rates? What sort of contracts do they expect owners to sign?

7. **Marketing** – what outlets are there to market and advertise properties? Would you be handling this side of things yourself, and if not how much do the alternatives cost?

8. **Seasonal effects** – if you are thinking of letting to tourists, how long is the season and how low do off-peak rates go? Does the high season coincide with when you would want to use a property? If letting long-term, for how long do properties lie vacant between tenants?

9. **Insurance** – what arrangements would you make for buildings and contents insurance, and how much would they cost, taking into account the fact your property would be let out?

10. **Maintenance** – how much would it cost to equip and furnish a property adequately? How frequently would you have to redecorate and replace items due to wear and tear?

Own use only

If you are looking for somewhere solely for your own use, you may have the freedom to look more off the beaten track or at more quirky properties. Because income generation is less of a driver, you may have the luxury of being able to afford the extra time and hassle of renovating somewhere.

Investment apartments

Apartments in major cities and provincial capitals can be a good buy if you are simply looking for an investment – generally speaking long-term tenancies are the best approach if what you want is regular, predictable income; although in some cities the 'city break' market means holiday lettings can be profitable. Properties close to universities and business parks often perform well. Wherever you look, you will want to see firm evidence of likely yields and capital growth – and of their sustainability – before getting into the nitty-gritty of searching for a particular property.

Choosing a property

Once you have decided on your preferred location, it is time to look at specific properties. You will probably do this with the help of an estate agent. This chapter gives advice on how to choose an agent, how much to pay them, what to look for during viewings and how to negotiate with owners.

Dealing with estate agents

Estate agents are a useful way of finding property abroad, but they can be expensive – for buyers as well as sellers, for both parties pay fees in some countries. Make sure you get good service and avoid unscrupulous sharks by checking credentials carefully before you proceed.

Having thought through your choice of area in a well-reasoned and objective way, it is important to retain the same level of lucidity when working towards finding the specific property that could, if you buy it, take up so much of your time, energy and financial resources.

There are no end of people keen to sell you overseas properties – from individual sellers to sales agents representing one or more property developers, to estate agents and property finders who can search the whole market on your behalf. But bear in mind that all of them stand to gain if you do go ahead and buy, regardless of whether the property is right for you. So it is up to you to make sure you manage the search process in a way that brings you a successful result.

ESTATE AGENTS' WEBSITES

Your first encounter with overseas estate agents may occur well before you arrange to leave Britain's shores for exploratory visits. Using estate agents' websites to help you find locations worth exploring – and even to help you find specific properties that might fit your criteria – can be a great way to start your search.

Using one of the main internet search engines and entering simple terms like 'estate agents' and the name of an area you want to find out about will often throw up a selection of property websites. Magazine and newspaper articles often quote estate agents' names and contact details, too.

Many overseas property websites feature an impressive range of properties; some provide useful information about the areas featured; most also include standard forms

> **! Estate agents on the internet**
>
> It is only the larger, international agencies or expatriate British agents marketing themselves to a British audience that bother to pay specialist web design firms to ensure their names appear high on lists compiled by search engines.

through which you can request property information to match your requirements.

It is worth bearing in mind that by no means all the agents selling properties in any given area will have a web presence. Often it is only the larger, international agencies, or expatriate British agents marketing themselves specifically to a British audience, that bother to pay specialist web design firms to ensure their names appear high on lists compiled by search engines. Some also promote themselves to journalists producing articles on the overseas property market for national newspapers, magazines and specialist publications.

Often local agents – even the overseas equivalents of our major high street estate agencies – do not market themselves actively to foreign buyers; or they may negotiate deals with international or UK-based agents to advertise some of their properties on their behalf.

Sometimes agents promoting just a small selection of purpose-built developments, rather than a more wide-ranging portfolio, will have impressive-looking websites and other marketing material targeted specifically at foreign buyers. They are likely to be either employed directly by the developers who built the properties, or be on contract to them, though – so be aware that their goal is to sell you a particular property or type of properties, rather than to search widely for somewhere that meets your needs.

Some web-based agencies specialise in investment properties, often focusing on particular sectors of the market, like whatever are the 'emerging markets' of the moment.

> **❝ No matter how much web-based research you have done, it is well worth pounding the streets of the area itself and making contact with local agents as well. ❞**

Another type of agency you may encounter is property-finder companies, which specialise in searching for properties that meet foreign clients' needs – the concept being that they will cut down the legwork for you and use their expert local knowledge to oversee the whole purchase, from property search to signing of the title deed, on your behalf.

No matter how much web-based research you have done into different agencies, it is well worth pounding

Estate agents' qualifications vary from country to country. For further details, see pages 59-61 and also look at the relevant section in Chapter 8.

the streets of the area itself and making contact with local agents as well. The wider you cast your net, the more likely you are to find a property that fits the bill; using local agents can also cut costs as you can avoid having to pay an intermediary.

CHECKING AGENTS' CREDENTIALS

Wherever you are looking for property, it is sensible to establish that the estate agents who might be working for you are properly qualified and accredited.

Particularly in areas where a significant share of the market is taken up by properties aimed at second home owners, like the Spanish costas and newer locations like Bulgaria's Black Sea coast, sales agents especially are very keen to sell to buyers from the UK and other north European countries.

It would be fair to say that a proportion of them see foreigners as relatively uninformed consumers, who are easy prey and hold out the prospect of hefty commissions for precious little effort.

Sales agents promoting specific developers do not have the monopoly on bad practice, though. It is not unknown for fraudsters posing as property sellers or estate agents to fleece unsuspecting second home hunters (see box).

There are several ways to protect yourself against crooks:

- Consult a range of agents and view a wide selection of properties, rather than putting yourself in the hands of one company. This should reduce your chances of being ripped off.
- Check the credentials of everyone you deal with, and make it clear that you are doing so, in order to drive the point home that you are not to be messed with (see right).
- Wherever possible, make use of any friends or contacts you have who are native or at least fluent speakers of the language; if not, pay for a good translator who can act as intermediary and, through their experience of how things should work locally, may be able to help you spot bad apples.

Property buying frauds

There are various scams that you need to be aware of before embarking on buying a property overseas, even through an agent. Although these shouldn't put you off, it is better to be forewarned about them so you can prevent crooks from ripping you off.

- Agent offers to hold your deposit while the sale goes through, then disappears with the money
- Agent inflates the sales price for foreign buyers, advertising the property at a higher price than the seller expects and pocketing the difference themselves
- Property 'owner' offers to sell you a property 'under the counter' to avoid red tape and tax – in fact, legally speaking you have bought nothing and they disappear with whatever money you have handed over

The strength of regulation of estate agents varies between countries, making it easier to identify rogue traders in some countries than others.

In much of western Europe and in the US there are qualifications that many, if not all, estate agents are expected to have; there are also representative bodies, registration with which confers added respectability.

France

All agents should be professionally qualified and hold a *carte professionnelle*, which should be displayed in their offices. They should also give details of their indemnity insurance and a bond or *piece de garantie*, which guarantees that if they were to run off with your deposit, you would get your money back. The three official estate agency bodies are the *Federation Nationale des Agents Immobiliers et Mandataires*, the *Syndicat Nationales des Professionels Immobilier* and the *Union Nationale de l'Immobilier*.

The absence of a *carte professionnelle* does not necessarily mean you are dealing with a crook, particularly if the agent in question is a British agent catering specifically for the UK market and acting on behalf of a French agent – although the latter scenario does not in itself offer any

❝A proportion of agents see foreigners as relatively uninformed consumers who are easy prey.❞

guarantee of good intentions. Similarly the absence of a *piece de garantie* need not necessarily set alarm bells ringing – it could simply be that the agent has chosen not to provide a deposit-holding facility for clients.

But in both cases the agent should be able to provide a reasonable explanation of why they do not have such documents; and it should be made crystal clear to you that under

Jargon buster

French	English
les arrhes	the deposit
agent immobilier	estate agent
bilan de santé	structural survey
carte professionnelle	agent's licence
expert immobilier	surveyor
mandat exclusif	sole selling rights
mandat simple	non-exclusive selling rights
piece de garantie	agent's bond
à vendre	for sale

For details of how to contact estate agents in a particular country, see the relevant 'Finding professionals' section in Chapter 8.

no circumstances would they hold your deposit money, which should be lodged with a properly bonded lawyer or notary instead.

Spain

There are two bodies which accredit agents; the *Gestores Intermediarios en Promociones de Edificaciones* and the *Agentes de la Propiedad Inmobilaria.*

Portugal

Look for a state-licensed agent or *mediador autorizado*, who should be able to show you their AMI number. The main professional body is the *Associação dos Profissionais das Empresas de Mediação Imobiliária de Portugal.*

Italy

All bona fide agents should be listed in a register or *ruoli* at the local chamber of commerce. If you are buying in one of the larger cities, you may want to use a *borsa immobiliari* – a free, centralised database run by larger chambers of commerce, which lists property for sale through accredited estate agents.

The relevant professional bodies are the *Federazione Italiana degli Agenti Immobiliari Professionali* and the *Federazione Italiana dei Mediatori e Agenti in Affari.*

Florida

Anyone who deals in real estate must be licensed, although agents who are employed directly by a single developer or builder need not be licensed. If you use a UK-based agent, they will not normally be licensed in Florida, which is not a reason to avoid them but do make sure the agents they are dealing with in Florida are themselves licensed.

Real estate agents, brokers or salespeople should be state licensed,

Jargon buster

Spanish	English	Italian	English
agents de fincas	estate agents	acconto	deposit
agrimensor	surveyor	agente immobiliare	estate agent
arras	deposit	consulente immobiliare	valuer
inspección	survey	geometra	surveyor/architect
notario	notary	in vendita	for sale
se vende	for sale	provvigione	estate agent's commission
		rogito	purchase deed
Portuguese	**English**	ruoli	register of licensed estate agents
mediador autorizado	state licensed		held at the Chamber of Commerce
	estate agent		(Camera di Commercio)
notano	notary	visura ipotecaria	credit search

which means they will have passed exams and are covered by indemnity insurance – this would compensate you for losses brought about by their errors or omissions. All licensed agents must conform to a code of practice set out by the Florida Real Estate Commission. Ask to see licenses – if the agent is a professional, this should cause no embarrassment whatsoever.

If you want to protect yourself still further, go for an agent or broker with the title 'realtor'. To use this term, a realtor must be a member of a local real estate board affiliated to the National Association of Realtors, which has a code of ethics; to be a member, they must have completed a course of study. Being able to complain to the NAR if necessary gives you another layer of protection.

The US equivalent of a property-finder agency is the 'buyer's broker' – that is, a real estate agent whom you employ to find you a property. There are several ways for a buyer's broker to make his or her money – they may charge you a fee, for example, or they may charge you nothing and

Check your estate agent's mandate

Sellers can appoint a single estate agent to sell their property, or can place it with a number of agencies; in some cases, for example in France, the latter approach may mean the seller also retains the right to sell the property him or herself.

It is beneficial for you to know which approach has been chosen, if only so you are aware that there could be other buyers viewing the property through a competitor agency.

In Florida, agents may be employed solely by either the buyer or the seller, which is called a 'single agency' arrangement; alternatively, an agent can work for both the buyer and seller – this is 'dual agency'; or they can work as an independent intermediary – 'transactional agency'.

Under Florida law a broker must disclose in writing on what basis he or she is acting, and it is vital to take note of this. Crucially, a broker acting on a 'single agency' or 'dual agency' basis must disclose all relevant information to their client, whereas one working as a 'transactional agency' only has a duty of honesty and fair dealing.

What this means is that if you make an enquiry or offer and are talking to an agent who is working for the seller (even if they are also working for you on a 'dual agency' basis), by law he or she must report everything you say – so play your cards close to your chest or the seller may find out what your top price is!

61

negotiate with the seller or their broker to split the seller's commission.

Wherever you are searching for property, responsible agents should have no problem showing you proof of their credentials; many will have relevant certificates displayed on the walls of their office, or on letterheads. If you are in any doubt about the veracity of such documents, ask for further clarification and if necessary, contact the awarding bodies to establish what protection, if any, they offer.

International estate agency bodies

The following bodies can be helpful sources of contact information about national representative organisations:

FIABCI
Countries covered: Europe/Africa: Andorra, Austria, Belgium, Bulgaria, Cyprus, Czech Republic, Denmark, Finland, France, Georgia, Germany, Greece, Hungary, Ireland, Israel, Italy, Latvia, Luxembourg, Monaco, Netherlands, Nigeria, Norway, Portugal, Russia, Slovenia, South Africa, Spain, Sweden, Switzerland, Tanzania, Turkey, UK; Americas: Argentina, Brazil, Canada, Cayman Islands, Colombia, Costa Rica, Dominican Republic, Mexico, Panama, Paraguay, US, Uruguay; Asia/Pacific: Australia, India, Indonesia, Japan, Korea, Malaysia, Philippines, Singapore, Thailand
Website: www.fiabci.com
Postal address: FIABCI Secretariat, 23 avenue Bosquet, 75007 Paris, France
Telephone: 00 33 1 4550 4549

ICREA
Countries covered: Argentina, Australia, Brazil, Canada, Czech Republic, Denmark, Finland, France, Greece, India, Ireland, Italy, Mexico, Netherlands, New Zealand, Norway, Poland, Portugal, Russia, Spain, Sweden, UK, US, Venezuela
Website: www.icrea.org
Central office contactable by email via the website

CEI
Countries covered: Austria, France, Germany, Greece, Hungary, Ireland, Italy, Netherlands, Portugal, Romania, Slovakia, Spain, UK. Affiliate members: Slovenia, Czech Republic
Website: http://webcei.com
Postal address: CEI, VBO (CEI) PO Box 17330, 2502 CH – The Hague, Netherlands
Telephone: 00 31 70 345 87 03

Relevant contact details for estate agency bodies in many of the countries you are likely to be searching in are shown in chapter 8.

If you are buying in Europe and it is not clear which national organisations agents should be members of, you may find it helpful to get in touch with the Confederation Europeenne d'Immobilier (CEI), a pan-European body which represents more than 25,000 estate agency professionals in 13 countries. The CEI acts as an umbrella organisation for individual countries' national organisations and operates a code of conduct for all member agencies.

Wider international estate agency networks include the International Real Estate Federation (FIABCI) and International Consortium of Real Estate Agents (ICREA), and these can be helpful sources of contact information about national representative bodies (see box).

In the UK, the Federation of Overseas Property Developers, Agents and Consultants (FOPDAC) represents estate agents, property developers and specialist consultants (including lawyers and mortgage brokers) who are active in the overseas property market. The organisation, which has existed since 1973, says its members must subscribe to a strict code of

Professional standards

The Association of Independent Property Professionals was launched in March 2006, with the aim of improving professional standards in the overseas property market. It has a strict code of conduct, insists on member companies having indemnity insurance and offers consumer advice. For contact details, see page 216.

conduct, running their businesses 'in a manner which seeks to protect the interests of those who have decided to purchase, or sell, a property overseas. Membership is restricted to companies or individuals whose probity is beyond reasonable question.' Its website, www.fopdac.co.uk, includes a list of members and their contact details.

Wherever you buy, you may of course encounter an agent with whom you feel you have a rapport and who does not have any of the relevant accreditation – perhaps because you are searching for a property in an emerging market and have found an enterprising British expatriate who is selling to UK buyers.

So long as you do not pay them any money until you have received a satisfactory service from them – and do not lodge any deposits or other monies with them – you may be happy

 For more details of estate agents in individual countries see chapter 8. Note that commission rates vary and that fees are often split between buyer and seller.

to deal with them. If so, use your common sense and operate on a 'buyer beware' basis.

ESTATE AGENTS' FEES

One nasty shock waiting for British people buying overseas is the fact that estate agents' fees – which are usually higher than we are used to – are borne, at least in part, by the buyer in some areas.

Fees vary considerably between countries, and even regionally, so it is vital to check details of fees at the outset or you could be in for an unwelcome surprise.

> " It is vital to check details of fees at the outset of negotiations or you could be in for an unwelcome surprise. "

If you buy in France, for example, you can expect to pay an estate agent anything from 4% to 12%, depending on the value of the property and whether buyers pay the full fee or it is split with the seller. In Spain sellers in tourist areas like the Costa Blanca and Costa del Sol often have to pay between 6% and 10%, and try to pass these costs on to buyers through higher house prices. Italian agents often ask for 3% each from buyer and seller.

In Florida buyers generally pay 6%, although because most properties are advertised across a shared 'multiple listing service', this fee is often shared between different agencies.

If you buy anywhere through a UK-based or other intermediary agent, they should generally earn their commission from the local agent whom they represent. But property-finder agents are likely to charge you commission, either at a fixed rate or 1-2% of the purchase price.

Perhaps unsurprisingly, the proportion of property advertised privately in countries where fees are expensive for sellers, is considerably higher than in the UK. It is estimated that around a fifth of all property transactions in Spain go through without estate agents being involved, for example. Particularly in rural areas of France, Spain and Italy, many sellers also advertise properties obliquely through their local notary to avoid high agency fees.

As a buyer it is well worth making clear to estate agents that you expect nothing less than complete transparency about the commissions they are charging. This can uncover bad practice among agents – it has been known for buyers to find out at the point of signing the final deed

Jargon buster

Multiple listing service A computer-based system for relaying information to real-estate agents about properties for sale.

that the price the agent has given them for the property is as much as a third higher than the price the seller will receive.

BRIEFING ESTATE AGENTS

Once you have pinpointed locations that interest you, thought about which kind of property might suit you best and satisfied yourself that your estate agent or agents are not con artists, your next step will be to set up some viewings.

But to be sure that when you contact estate agents you stand a good chance of finding properties that meet your requirements, draw up a list of criteria that you want potential properties to fulfil beforehand. This will help you brief agents much more effectively, enabling you to be clear about which are the non-negotiable aspects of your wish list, and which are more flexible.

Armed with your previous homework, start with a blank sheet of paper and write down what you would like your property to be like, taking into account the constraints of your budget and the kind of properties you know to be on offer in the localities in which you are interested. How many bedrooms would you want it to have? Is outside space important to you? How near must it be to everyday conveniences like shops and restaurants? What would be the maximum distance from an airport that you or your clients could stomach?

Examples of property criteria

Holiday home plus lettings

1. Must have at least three bedrooms
2. Must have a swimming pool or pool access, plus a garden
3. No more than an hour from airport
4. Less than half an hour from beach
5. Prefer an established lettings record
6. Prefer shops and restaurants within 15 mins' walking distance

Investment property

1. Must be in one of two or three particular, named districts
2. Prefer two bedrooms
3. Lift access essential
4. Service charge no more than defined amount per month
5. Must have secure parking space
6. No sitting tenants

Retirement property

1. Enough bedrooms to accommodate visiting family
2. Must have easy access to golf course, preferably on site
3. Prefer garden (not too large)
4. Close to town, including doctor and pharmacist
5. No more than 90 minutes from airport
6. Quiet neighbourhood, preferably retired neighbours

Viewing properties

Viewing properties overseas is fundamentally the same as viewing properties in the UK, and it is helpful to be as thorough as possible on these valuable fact-finding visits. Always take your time and approach the task exactly as you would if you were viewing in the UK.

Especially if you are viewing properties in a rural area, resist the temptation to 'go it alone' and conduct your own viewings without the agent being present – partly for safety reasons and partly because you could easily get lost and end up seeing far fewer properties than you had planned, and irritate sellers in the process.

Bear in mind that foreign properties can be very different from what you are used to in the UK and that it is easy for your judgement to be clouded as a result. Sunshine, sea views and, especially if you are looking at old properties, the romance of charmingly un-British buildings can all contribute to muddled thinking.

Quality of building materials, and the size of properties and land, can be very different from what we are used to the in UK.

On the plus side, in modern buildings, internal walls are more likely to be made of brick rather than plasterboard on a wooden frame, and marble floors and worktops are much less prohibitively expensive, for example. In older properties, you may be faced with beautiful solid wooden doors, antique tiles, quaint shutters and enough outbuildings to house a small army.

On the minus side, building quality can be very variable, depending on the age and location of the building and the extent to which it was built in compliance with building regulations. If the property is very run-down and does not have access to mains electricity and water, bear in mind that the costs of connecting these can be prohibitively high. Installing or bringing septic tanks up to latest standards can also be expensive (see page 95).

When one takes into account the relatively low prices of many overseas properties, you may find that most of the places you view appear to be great value for money.

But remember that to be sure of finding a good buy, you need to be comparing properties not with their equivalent in the UK, but with the rest of the local market. Remember also that the ramshackle look you find appealing now might translate into high maintenance costs, and end up being a total turn-off for future buyers.

If at all possible, take a trusted native speaker with you on viewings, to help you pose questions to the agent and, if they are present, the seller; and to interpret the answers (see box on page 72). Taking someone who knows a lot about buildings can also be a sensible precaution, although bear in mind that construction techniques in other countries can be very different from those used in the UK.

Look for visible defects, because in some countries sellers are not obliged by law to disclose anything that you could have discovered for yourself when viewing the property; hidden

"Building quality can be very variable, depending on the age and location of the building. "

defects must be disclosed, although of course canny sellers will have done their best to disguise these.

View properties in daylight, and if you are impressed, arrange for a second visit at a different time of day – perhaps at rush hour, or on a Sunday, to get a better feel for how the surroundings change throughout the week.

Habitable vs ruin

There are pros and cons to buying a ruin. For some a restored or newly built property may be more suitable.

Habitable		Ruin	
Pros	Cons	Pros	Cons
Less demanding of your time	Less scope to stamp your mark on the property and increase capital as a result	You get to choose how you want the property to be done	Renovation costs may spiral
Could produce income immediately	Has not been designed with you in mind	Generally cheap	Could take a huge amount of time and effort
Costs are more predictable	More expensive than somewhere to restore	Value could rise disproportionately thanks to the work you have done	No income until refurbishment complete

Property measurements

In Europe and elsewhere, it is typical for properties' size in square metres to be advertised. Such figures may initially hold little meaning for you, so here is a rough idea of what they equate to:

50 square metres	=	one-bedroom apartment, small cottage
75 square metres	=	two-bedroom apartment or terraced house
100 square metres	=	large two-bedroom apartment or modern three-bedroom semi-detached
150 square metres	=	four-bedroom detached house

If you are having a survey done, ask the surveyor to check the measurements carefully, as they are not always accurate.

If you buy wisely you may be able to find a property that would also appeal to local buyers, thus increasing your likelihood of getting a good price Doing plenty of homework before you view the property – for example finding out about average wage rates and availability of mortgage finance for locals – should help you establish how wide a market your property could have in future.

Even if you only plan to use the property for holidays and/or holiday lettings, try to ask the kind of questions a permanent resident might need answers to, thus anticipating what future buyers might want to know from you.

VIEWING OFF-PLAN DEVELOPMENTS

Many foreign buyers go down the route of buying overseas properties 'off plan', which means committing to buy at some point between the developers' plans being approved by the local authorities, and the last brick being laid.

The advantage of this is that prices are set lower than would be the case if you were buying a completed property, to compensate you for the inconvenience of having to wait for it, and the rest of the development, to be finished.

One of the biggest issues when you view properties should be how easy or otherwise it would be to sell the property when the time comes.

In some areas, for example where property is cheap by UK standards but too expensive for local people to afford, your market could be restricted mainly or exclusively to other second home buyers – which may become problematic if changes to the UK economy lead to fewer people investing overseas.

 In France, there are clear rules about advance payments when buying unfinished properties. Other countries are less well regulated. Be particularly wary of agreeing staged payments on set dates regardless of progress. See pages 92-3 for further details.

It may be tempting to think that if the property you are thinking of buying does not even exist yet, it would be pointless to arrange a viewing – and developers in many markets popular with investors, including Turkey, Bulgaria and Brazil, report that a surprising number of people do, indeed, buy without even seeing the development.

Failing to visit the development can be a huge mistake, though. The absence of finished buildings creates plenty of scope for glossy marketing material that stretches the boundaries of credibility. Artists' impressions of completed developments can look considerably more impressive than the real thing – especially if the artist neglected to sketch in the flyover that runs within 200 yards of the complex, or the sea view that is about to be obscured by an enormous skyscraper.

Off-plan vs resale

It is worth weighing up the advantages and disadvantages of buying a property before it has been completed.

Off-plan		Resale	
Pros	Cons	Pros	Cons
Could give better capital growth	Risk of developer going bust	May already have established rental/ lettings income	Depending on location and planning rules, may be lower build quality
Newer development so may have better facilities	Area may already be saturated with purpose-built properties	You can see the property as it is, rather than just on paper	Full purchase price required more quickly
Staged payments reduce immediate financial commitment	Risk of property and/or development falling below your expectations	Development and shared facilities, eg pools, more likely to be completed	May have fewer facilities than newer, more imaginative complexes
More choice over fixtures and fittings	Hassle of being surrounded by a building site, and effects of this on potential income	Easier purchase process, eg no requirement for developers' guarantees	Less choice over fixtures and fittings

Even if there are no walls, roof or internal fittings to inspect, visiting development sites can help you assess the pros and cons of the location, look in detail at where your property would be situated, assess progress to date and quiz agents in person about all aspects of the deal. For details on the host of legal issues to consider when thinking about buying an off-plan property, see chapter 4.

Inspection trips

Many sales agents and developers organise inspection trips, which purport to make life easier for property hunters. Typically they will involve a long weekend of intensive property viewings in a pre-arranged set of locations, and will be organised along the lines of a package coach tour – complete with free drinks parties and introductions to developers, lawyers, architects and the like.

Such visits are often cheap – less than £250 for a long weekend, including accommodation – but the focus of the trip is usually just one or two resorts, and often more specifically one or a number of developments in the process of being marketed.

Even if the sales team are slick enough to make their marketing appear subtle – and often they are not – rest assured that the pay-off for all that hospitality is the expectation that you will commit to buying something. If you do go on an inspection trip, tread carefully and do not sign any

paperwork until you have had it checked by a properly qualified, independent lawyer.

NEGOTIATING WITH THE SELLER

Perhaps the most crucial difference between buying property in England and Wales and buying property just about anywhere else in the world is that elsewhere, there is no such thing as a non-binding offer.

In England and Wales it is possible to make an offer on a house and never get anywhere near exchange of contracts. Weeks or even months can pass, during which searches are carried out, mortgages arranged and surveys done.

Even if both parties have agreed with their respective representatives that they want to go ahead with the transaction, only once all the details are ironed out does anyone move to formally commit to their respective sides of the bargain, apart from paying a few initial fees.

Indeed, before contracts are exchanged, buyers in England and Wales may even make speculative offers on a number of properties, before they have properly decided which property to go for – and then disappear off into the sunset.

Particularly if the buyer knows that the seller is in a rush to sell, they may identify aspects of a property that they are not happy with early on, but not bother to negotiate a reduction in price accordingly until a point where

20 issues to focus on when viewing properties

1. Accessibility

2. Proximity to local amenities

3. Overall size of accommodation (see page 68 for tips on measurements)

4. Layout, shape and position of rooms – even in spacious properties it is possible to have a lot of wasted space, oddly shaped rooms that you cannot fit furniture into, and strange layouts, for example bedrooms coming off living rooms or the main bathroom coming off one of the bedrooms.

5. Structure of the property

6. Plumbing and electrics – check water pressure by turning on taps in the upstairs bathroom and testing the shower, for example

7. Heating and air conditioning – check what type of boiler there is, look at the size and position of radiators and find out how many rooms have air conditioning

8. Built-in storage space – is there enough of it, or too much, and is it in useful places?

9. Natural light

10. Views and position in relation to sun

11. Size, shape and position of outside space

12. Parking – if there is no parking space included, what are your alternatives and how much would they cost? Especially if you are buying a city apartment to rent out, this could be a deal-breaker

13. Noise and soundproofing, which could be especially important if you are buying in an urban area near to bars or clubs, for example

14. Scope for expansion within the building – look at how easy it would be to 'remodel' the property by moving rooms around, and whether there are cellars and lofts that could be used to create more space

15. Outbuildings or space for extensions – might it be possible to renovate a separate building or add some rooms, to help generate extra income?

16. Quality of fixtures and fittings – these could be essential if you are planning to let the property to upmarket clients

17. Proximity to neighbours

18. State of internal and external décor

19. Proximity to the sea – the nearer it is, the better a rental price it is likely to command

20. Facilities shared with neighbours – look at how well designed and maintained they are, how much use they seem to get and the overall atmosphere of the development

Some questions to ask on viewings

- What does the price include and exclude? Sometimes there may be outbuildings which are being sold separately, threatening your splendid isolation; if you are buying an investment apartment, being able to buy it fully furnished may be an attraction.
- Is the property offered freehold or leasehold? If the latter, what is the ground rent, how long is the lease, who owns the freehold and is there the option to buy it?
- Are there any tenants living at the property, and if so will it be sold with vacant possession? If not you will need to be very careful about your legal rights to end the tenancy.
- Are there any restrictive covenants on the lease, for example about ownership of pets or use of facilities by children? These can be surprisingly harsh and may be enough to make you think again about the whole deal.
- What service charges are there? You will need to find out what work the management company has planned and at what cost, and to see their previous works schedule – the more information you can get at this stage, the better.
- Where are the boundaries of the property? Bear in mind that these may not be obvious from the position of fences or hedges.
- If there is a well, what are the ownership rights? Wells can be a valuable resource, if only for water to use on the garden; but for historical reasons other people may have rights of way to use your well.
- Does the property have mains electricity, gas and drainage? If not, how close is it to these services? Bear in mind that the costs of connection could be high.
- If there is a septic tank, does this comply with the current regulations?
- Are there any structural problems?
- What, if any, building work has been done by the existing owners – and is any of this work covered by guarantees?
- Does the property have planning permission for further work, or are there restrictions on what can be done to the building and/or land?
- Does anyone else have rights of way over the land?
- Is the area prone to flooding? If so this could raise your insurance premiums sky high, not to mention having the potential to cause huge damage to your house and belongings.
- Has the property been tested for asbestos, termites and lead?
- How quickly do the owners want to sell? Is there a chain? Such issues could affect what price they will accept, or if you would only consider buying after securing planning permission, could put you off altogether.
- What are the local schools like? Even if this is of no interest to you personally, it could be crucial to whoever buys from you in the future; being located near to an excellent school could be a big selling point.
- What are the neighbours like? Your enjoyment of the property could be seriously affected by the people next door, for example if they are unfriendly towards foreigners, make a lot of noise or happen to be the local drug dealer.
- If the property is let out to tenants or tourists, what income does it produce and are letting records available? If you can take over a property where there is clear evidence of people wanting to let it, your life could be an awful lot easier.

the seller – having progressed their buying of another property – has no option but to agree.

In most other countries, the expectation is that if you are serious about buying a property, you will move quickly to agree a contract; and that once the seller has agreed to sell you the property, you are both as committed to the deal – and the price agreed – as you would be at exchange of contracts in England and Wales.

Agreeing a contract before searches and surveys are carried out and mortgage applications completed may seem foolhardy, but as shown in chapter 4, a well drafted contract will allow you to get out of the deal if any aspects of the transaction prove problematic.

Having said this, if the property you are looking at appears to be in poor shape, it may be sensible to insist on having a survey done before you progress to agreeing a contract – if not

‹‹ If the property appears to be in poor shape, it may be sensible to insist on having a survey done before agreeing to a contract. ››

as a way to negotiate a drop in price, than at least to reassure yourself that the problems with the property are not so great as to put you off the whole deal.

Sellers in many parts of continental Europe can get a bit sniffy about this, because there is much less of a tradition of pre-purchase surveys than is the case in the UK – and many will insist on keeping the property on the market until you are ready to sign contracts. But if having a survey done before agreeing to buy is important to you, stand your ground. For more

Ten questions to ask about the asking price

1 Is it fair in comparison to similar properties in the area?
2 Can you afford it?
3 How strong is the market - are there other people who might pay the full price?
4 Do you want the property so much you would pay over the odds for it?
5 If the seller refused to drop the price, would you walk away?
6 Would you be prepared to meet the seller somewhere in the middle?
7 Is there scope to add value to the property?
8 How much would you have to spend on renovations/improvements?
9 Are you torn between this and another property?
10 Are you happy that you have seen all the properties you need to?

Getting ready to agree a contract

If you are happy with the property and the price, make a list of issues arising from your contacts with the seller and agent, to raise with your lawyer when drawing up an initial contract – which will set out in detail the agreement between you and the seller.

You should find that a good lawyer will cover most of your concerns in the drafting of the preliminary contract, but it pays to be thorough, so that nothing slips through the net. Your list might include issues such as whether or not planning permission was granted for refurbishment work at the property; questions over access to a well, or rights of way; and what you have been told about who pays for the estate agent.

You should also be ready to provide details of how far advanced you are in terms of raising mortgage finance, if necessary; and you should be clear about whose name will go on the title deeds. For further details on agreeing contracts, see Chapter 4.

details on arranging a survey, see pages 94-5.

Survey or no survey, it is vital to be happy with the price of the property before progressing to the stage of agreeing a contract. So if you are not, you will need to ask your estate agent to put your case for a reduced price. It is up to you whether to reveal what your final top price might be upfront, so they have some room for manoeuvre; or whether to appear firm with your initial proposal.

As a second home buyer, you may have some advantages from a negotiating standpoint. You may be a cash buyer, for example if you are buying using an inherited lump sum, which could speed up the sale; even if not, you are unlikely to have to sell another property, which means that so long as your equity release or second mortgage comes through, the transaction is likely to go through smoothly.

Bear in mind, though, that depending on where you are buying and from whom, a proposed drop in price may be considered a personal insult and greeted with a Gallic shrug – so be prepared to either walk away, or return with a higher offer and be forced to consume a large slice of humble pie.

 In the case of older properties you may need a full survey before deciding to go ahead. You might also want an architect or builder to advise on restoration. See pages 94-5 for further details.

The buying process

The contractual arrangements for buying property abroad are different from those in the UK. Buyers are expected to sign a preliminary contract and pay a deposit at an earlier stage in the proceedings, so sound independent legal advice is crucial.

Buying abroad

Once you have found a property that you feel fulfils your needs, you are ready to move on to what might feel like the scariest part of owning an overseas property – the buying process. Stay alert and don't be shy about taking legal advice.

Language barriers and different sets of rules and regulations can make the whole experience seem alien, but with the right attitude and a sensible mix of qualified professionals around you, there is no reason why this all-important stage should not run as smoothly as you might expect it to in the UK. In fact, it might be much less stressful than you think.

FINDING A LAWYER

Even before you start serious property hunting, it is advisable to consult a suitably qualified lawyer to talk about the likely impact of an overseas property purchase on your overall legal and tax situation in the UK.

No matter what kind of property you buy, any second property will be a considerable addition to your estate, and it is important to decide how best to handle the purchase in principle, from the point of view of inheritance and other taxes across the two jurisdictions.

Choose a lawyer who has experience of dealing with overseas property transactions in the country or countries you are thinking of buying in – or has access to colleagues with such experience – rather than just appointing a standard high street firm.

You may wish to appoint an English-speaking lawyer based in the country you are buying in, but you will need to make sure they understand your overall legal and tax situation in both countries, so they can structure the purchase accordingly. You may prefer to engage a UK-based lawyer who specialises in overseas property work; depending on the complexity of your circumstances you may even want both, especially since you will need to make new wills in both countries, to take into account the new asset.

To find a lawyer in the UK who specialises in overseas property work,

 In most European countries property transactions are overseen by public officials known as notaries. They are an impartial safeguard but no substitute for your own lawyer. See page 86 for further details.

you may want to ask for recommendations from friends and family – especially any who have bought overseas.

Another source is the Law Society, which has a searchable database of solicitors working in England and Wales, accessible via its website, www.lawsociety.org.uk. The database also allows you to search for English-qualified lawyers who do work overseas, by country; a separate, printed *Directory of Solicitors and Barristers* lists those who practise entirely outside England and Wales. The Law Society also keeps a separate list of foreign-qualified lawyers working in England and Wales, although because these lawyers

"Choose a lawyer who has experience of dealing with overseas property transactions in the country or countries you are thinking of buying in."

qualified in their own countries, they are not regulated by the Law Society.

A small number of lawyers who specialise in overseas property law are members of the Federation of Overseas Property Developers, Agents and Consultants, and their contact details can be found through its website, www.fopdac.co.uk.

Criteria for choosing a lawyer

When buying property abroad you need to give special consideration to which lawyer you should use to handle your purchase. The fact that you are buying overseas and dealing in a foreign language means that your lawyer's expertise and experience is even more important than the property-buying process back home.

These are the key points to look for:

- Expertise in overseas real estate

- Good understanding of needs of non-resident buyers

- Bilingual service

- Fees, which should normally be in the region of 1-2% of the purchase price

- Friendly, helpful and proactive manner

- Established systems for dealing with buyers not based in the country

The easiest way to find an English-speaking lawyer in an overseas country is to go through the British Embassy in that country. The Foreign and Commonwealth Office website, www.fco.gov.uk, lists British embassies, consulates and other diplomatic missions in countries all over the world, and in many cases provides links to embassies' own websites.

At the very least these provide contact details for embassy staff, and at best they list names and contact

> " Be wary of recommendations from developers or their sales agents. "

details for English-speaking lawyers, or firms where lawyers' assistants can translate. Choose 'UK embassies overseas' from the drop-down menu at the top of the opening page of the FCO site to search for the information you want.

If you have friends or family in the area you plan to buy in, you may want to ask them for recommendations; trusted estate agents may also be able to help, but be wary of recommendations from developers or their sales agents – it is important to have paperwork handled by a genuinely independent legal professional.

BRIEFING YOUR LAWYER

At your initial meeting with your lawyer, you will need to give them plenty of information about who you are, where you come from and what services you want them to provide. They will want details of your estate agent and the property you are interested in, and you should show them any documentation you have about the property, which may – especially if you are buying a new or off-plan property – include a pre-prepared preliminary contract provided by the estate agent.

They should ask you questions about why you want to buy the property, whether you are borrowing money to finance the purchase and what stage you are at with mortgage applications. They will also need to know which notary will be handling the transaction (see page 90).

You may have particular issues you wish to raise with them, arising from your viewings and dealings with the estate agent, and you will need to discuss what you expect of each other in terms of ongoing communication, and your presence at the signing of the final deed.

 Land grab

If you are buying in the Valencia region of Spain, tread carefully or you could fall foul of laws that allow developers to sequester your land. Take legal advice. See page 164.

Key legal issues

As the buying process progresses there are several key issues you will need your lawyer to focus on. These range from contracts and 'get out' clauses to title deeds and planning permission. You will also need to consider your tax position and how to register ownership of the new property.

OWNERSHIP OF THE PROPERTY

A big issue to think about when buying in some European countries, most notably France and Spain, is who should own the property, and how.

Failing to address this issue comprehensively from the start – by deciding whose name should go on the deeds and in what way, and making appropriate wills – could leave you in a situation where the property passes to the wrong people when you die, and where your heirs incur unnecessary and punitive inheritance tax bills.

Your choice of whose name should go on the title deeds is crucial if you are buying as a couple, as is your choice of 'matrimonial regime' – the framework under which married couples in many countries, including France, Spain and Italy, deal with their finances.

There are two types of matrimonial regime. One option is common ownership of assets, whereby all assets acquired after the marriage – even if they are put in one party's name – belong to both people. The other option is separate ownership, whereby each spouse is entitled to own assets in their own name, and the other has no automatic claim over them.

Decisions about which regime to go for; which of you should own the property if you opt for separate ownership; and which form of property ownership to go for (you could buy jointly as two individuals or buy jointly as an entity – known respectively as *en indivision* and *en tontine* in France; or buy through a company); have obvious tax implications, and can also make a big difference if you divorce or one of you dies.

If you opt for the separate ownership regime and buy a property *en indivision* in France and then die,

 Although the law relating to property ownership is broadly similar in most European countries, there are some significance differences, of which you need to be aware. For more details see the country-by-country entries in Chapter 8.

Setting up a company

In some parts of eastern Europe, the law states that individuals can own buildings but not land; to get round this, it is possible to set up a company in the country in question and buy the land through that. This normally costs a few hundred pounds and requires you to file annual reports. Take professional legal advice before following this course of action.

for example, your half will be disposed of according to fixed rules (see box).

A person who owns *en indivision* can also insist on the property being sold, even against the wishes of the other owner – so if, for example, you are a wicked step-parent, your

deceased partner's children, having inherited half the property, could have you out on your ear in next to no time!

If you buy *en tontine* – even if you operate under the separate ownership regime – your half will pass to the other joint owner automatically on your death.

Alternatively, you could go for common ownership and make a *clause d'attribution* that on your death the property passes to the other partner; he or she then becomes the owner and without needing to pay inheritance tax either – but only if you have no children by a previous relationship, and the heirs of the second partner will face a bigger inheritance tax bill as result.

Another option to consider if you

French inheritance laws

Assets disposed of under French inheritance law are split into a freely disposable part (*quotite disponible*) and a protected part (*reserve hereditaire*). The reserved part must be given to the following people:

- If you have one child of any age, your own or adopted, but not including step-children; or if your child, now deceased, left children – you must given them 50% of your total estate.
- If you have two children (as above) or a mixture of living and dead children who left children – they must have 66%.
- Three or more children (as above) must get 75%.
- If you have no children but you have a living parent or grandparent on one side, they must get 25% of the total estate (although this can be reduced to a life interest if you have a surviving spouse and your will specifies this).
- If you have no children but a living parent or grandparent on both sides, 25% of the total estate must go to each branch of the family (or as a life interest as above).

have adult children is to give them the money to buy part of the property and add them to the title. Tax-wise, this can – so long as you arrange it all properly so as to avoid gift tax – save you a lot of money because you only own a quarter, fifth or whatever of the property, instead of half; meaning only that part will be taxable.

An alternative is to put the property entirely in the names of your children but retain a life interest for yourselves. This would allow you to live there and only pass the property on after the two of you have died. Again, you would have to make sure this gift was administered properly so as to avoid gift tax. Bear in mind also that if your child or children died before you and without heirs, you could find yourself inheriting the property back and having to pay inheritance tax as a result!

It is not difficult to see that expert legal advice on all of this is vital; the complexity increases still further if you are not married, or are same-sex partners.

There are various other ways of owning property which can, in particular circumstances, be worth thinking about too. People buying in countries which restrict foreigners' ability to own land and/or property – including Bulgaria and Croatia – have got round the problem by setting up a company and buying through that, for example. Trusts, which are not recognised as legal entities in many European countries and can therefore

be useful tools for sheltering assets from tax, may also be an option.

Making sure such arrangements are watertight, beneficial and administratively not too onerous is a job best left to a suitably qualified lawyer.

❝ Your choice of whose name should go on the title deeds is absolutely crucial. ❞

CLEAN TITLE

Wherever you are buying, establishing that the person selling the property is actually its owner and has the right to sell is a key task, and one which you must entrust to a suitably qualified professional.

At a basic level, married people whose finances operate under common ownership cannot sell a property without the consent of their spouse, for example – but plenty try.

Title issues can be more problematic in parts of Eastern Europe in particular, where the combined effects of inheritance laws which encourage the splitting of assets between children; families dispersed by economic hardship; ownership disputes caused by appropriation of land during wartime; and unreliable land registry paperwork; mean that it can be a considerable legal challenge to prove clearly that the person selling

81

PLANNING ISSUES

In many parts of Europe, as in the UK, the planning rules administered by local authorities are extremely strict It is essential for your lawyer to check the planning status of the property at an early stage in proceedings, or at the very least to ensure that you do not have to buy the property if these searches prove problematic.

The way planning is organised varies between countries, but in essence all properties are defined by their local authorities as being located in a particular planning zone, and there will be clear rules about what kind of development can be done – and with what level of local authority control – in each zone.

In some heavily protected zones, property owners may not even be able to change their front doors without first consulting the authorities; in others the rules are much more relaxed; but there will always be a requirement to follow the rules and have documentation to prove that you have done so.

The most important thing is to find out whether your property is in a zone where, in principle, planning permission could be granted for you to undertake renovations, build extensions or make other additions to the property, such as building a

you the property is its undisputed owner.

Checking out whether other people have rights of way over any land you are buying, or whether they have 'pre-emption rights', is also crucial. In Italy if any of the land you are considering buying is designated as 'rural' – that is, agricultural – any neighbouring farmers must be given first refusal to buy it, for example. Once alerted to the fact the land is on the market, they have up to 30 days in which to register an interest; if they do not want it, your lawyer must ask them for written confirmation of that. Failure to do this can, within the first year of your ownership, result in a demand that you sell the land to them.

For more on Cyprus and the problems caused by the division of the island, see Chapter 8, page 183.

swimming pool. This could affect whether or not you want the property, and could affect its value dramatically – so you may need your lawyer's advice on how best to proceed if the news is not good.

There are other planning issues to consider, too. If you are buying a ruined agricultural building to renovate, the owner may have applied to the planning authorities for approval for a change of use, to allow the property to be used as a residence; if not you may need to delay buying it until such approval is granted, or make approval a condition of the sale.

And if the person selling you the property has done work that falls foul of the planning rules, fines will be due and your purchase contract must make clear that these will need to be paid before ownership passes to you.

CONTRACTS WITH DEVELOPERS

If you are buying off-plan, as many investors do, you need to be as confident as possible that the developer building your home is reputable. It makes sense to see

❝Your lawyer must ensure that the developer offers a bank guarantee. ❞

examples of the company's previous projects and try to establish what its track record is like before agreeing to buy. But you will need legal protection as well. Have your lawyer conduct searches as soon as possible, to satisfy yourself that the area surrounding the property is not about to be blighted by further building work; he or she must also negotiate clauses governing time of delivery.

Crucially, your lawyer must ensure that the developer offers a **bank guarantee**, meaning that even if they go bust, the bank will pay for the project to be completed. In Italy such bank guarantees are now mandatory, but elsewhere you may have to settle for a less comprehensive guarantee that only provides for you to get your money back; if you want to claim for damages if you have sustained a loss as a result, you will have to go through the courts.

When in Rome... use a geometra

A *geometra* is an Italian professional who in English terms is somewhere between a surveyor and an architect; he or she can project manage property renovations and is frequently employed to conduct planning and other local authority searches as part of the property buying process. The *collegio dei geometri* in each province holds details of all registered *geometri* in that area.

If the developer were to offer neither kind of guarantee, you could end up having spent all that money for an unfinished shell of a building – and needing to club together with the other owners to arrange for someone to finish the development.

" Once a reservation contract is signed you are fully committed to the purchase. "

It is vital to remember that, unlike in the UK, where it is common to pay a small, non-binding deposit to reserve an off-plan property, all this legal work must be done before you sign anything or hand over any money – once a reservation contract is signed you are fully committed to the purchase (see page 92).

LEASEBACK DEALS

Many UK investors are attracted by leaseback schemes, which are particularly popular in France and hold out the prospect of exemption from VAT on the purchase price, as well as hassle-free holiday home ownership, including a predictable monthly rental income and a fixed number of weeks' personal use per year.

But make sure your lawyer goes over all the documentation relating to the leaseback deal with a fine-tooth comb. While leaseback properties tend to be built by big developers, the lettings are often handled by a small firm, perhaps set up by a local estate agent. During the selling phase big claims are made for rental yields, but these may then prove unsustainable and either the firm goes bust or the yields have to be revised downwards. At the end of the leaseback the management firm may also write into the contract that it has an automatic right to renew the deal. Unless your lawyer negotiates different terms, you can be locked into a sub-standard deal whether you like it or not.

Bear in mind also that some lawyers with particular expertise in this field are able to negotiate VAT exemption through means other than a full-blown leaseback scheme.

Jargon buster

Off-plan guarantees
Bank guarantee (extrinsic guarantee) a bank will pay for the project to be completed if the original developer fails (see page 93)
Intrinsic guarantee no guarantee that project will be completed, only that you won't lose your investment (see page 93)

TAX

Wherever you buy, you will be liable for tax in the country in question; and, if there is no double taxation treaty with the UK, potentially back at home too. The levels of these taxes vary according to individual governments' fiscal policies and, in the case of foreign owners, the way the authorities choose to deal with non-resident owners.

For details on tax rates in individual countries, see Chapter 7, which includes the rates at the time of writing, along with contact details for government bodies from whom to glean the latest information.

The main taxes to concern yourself with are:

- **Purchase taxes** – payable on all property purchases.
- **Income tax** – payable on rental income.
- **Capital gains tax** – payable on profits from sales of second homes.
- **Inheritance and gift tax** – payable by heirs or gift recipients who receive assets including property.
- **Wealth taxes** – payable by high net worth individuals.

Your lawyer should be able to advise you on how best to handle your property purchase in terms of tax liabilities, but if your circumstances are complex you may also need to consult a specialist tax adviser.

CONDOMINIUM RULES

If you are buying in an apartment or villa complex, you will become part of a community of owners who share facilities beyond the boundaries of your own property – everything from roofs, foundations, lifts and corridors to entrance areas, car parks, swimming pools and shared gardens.

As well as being responsible for your own home, you will be responsible for a share of the community's expenses, for example to pay for maintenance of the swimming pool and common areas.

Your estate agent or the seller's notary should provide details of the service charge you must pay and the structure of the community's administration; you should also receive a copy of the community's rules – which may impose restrictions on times when the pool may be used, whether or not pets can be kept on the premises and even whether or not you can hang washing on your balcony.

If you are not happy with these rules, there may be little your lawyer can do to change them, but at the very least he or she will be able to explain what your responsibilities are.

RENTING THE PROPERTY OUT

If you are buying an investment property with a view to renting it out to permanent tenants, your lawyer should be able to advise you on how to handle this from a legal perspective.

In Florida in particular, in many parts of the state there are restrictions against people letting their properties

For more on renting out your property, and a consideration of the likely costs and returns, see Chapter 1, page 29 and Chapter 2, pages 52-4.

out on short-term rentals (a month or less); this can be more of an issue if you are buying in a condominium but whole areas can be 'zoned' so that tourist rents are not allowed. For more information on buying properties in Florida, see pages 178-81.

Laws relating to landlords and tenants vary by country, but it is fair to say that the standard short hold tenancy agreement in England and Wales is amongst the most liberal from the landlord's point of view.

In many countries there are tighter controls on rent levels, and it can be much more difficult to evict tenants, so you will need to bear your lawyer's advice in mind before agreeing to buy such a property.

THE ROLE OF THE NOTARY

In England and Wales, although you may never have thought about it this way, there are essentially two steps to buying a property – and although the detail and timing may be different, the same is true overseas.

Step one is negotiating a private contract between buyer and seller, specifying how much money is going to change hands and when, what is included in the sale and what happens if either party decides to pull out.

Step two formalises the fundamentals of that contract into an official document that registers the transaction from the point of view of public bodies like the Land Registry and tax authorities.

Notaries are public officials qualified in the civil law, who play a key part in the property purchase process in most of Europe (except the UK, Cyprus and Denmark). Their main role as far as you are concerned will be to handle step two of the process – that is, checking that that title deeds are in order, recording the sale, and ensuring that all the relevant public authorities receive whatever taxes they are owed.

In most cases the seller will probably suggest a notary to handle step two, and he or she will also provide much of the paperwork necessary for step one.

In preparation for step two, he or she will also duplicate some of the work your lawyer will do on your behalf – conducting searches to make sure there are no outstanding debts lodged against the property, for example, and looking carefully to make sure no-one else has a claim to ownership.

It is in fact possible – and, between locals, common – for property

To find a notary or check their credentials, contact their national representative body. The Conference des Notariats de l'Union Europeenne represents around 35,000 notaries in Austria, Belgium, France, Germany, Greece, Italy, Luxembourg, Netherlands, Portugal and Spain. Its website, www.cnue.be (which is mainly in French), has links to the national bodies.

Key issues to cover in a contrato privado

Although this checklist relates specifically to the most common form of preliminary contract in Spain, many of the issues it lists also apply to the compromis de vente in France and the compromesso in Italy. For more details of the buying process, see pages 88-93 and 98-106.

- That in legal terms, the property and its boundaries match what you think you are buying.
- That the people you are buying the property from are actually its owners, i.e. it is their names that appear on the local land register (registro de la propiedad); it is these people whose names should appear in the purchase contract.
- If there are any existing debts or mortgages against the property – these must be paid by the seller before legal ownership transfers to you, or they become your responsibility.
- That the proper planning consents have been sought, building regulations followed, fines paid and so on.
- Where you are buying a plot of land, that it is properly designated as land permitted to be developed.
- Exactly what is included in (and excluded from) the sale; issues about rights of way, etc.
- Pre-emption rights, for example if the vendor co-owns the property with someone else, who automatically has the right to buy it in preference to you.
- In the case of a new build, what the arrangements are for stage payments, completion dates and the like.

transactions to go through with only a notary involved; or for the buyer and seller to appoint separate notaries to conduct proceedings. In some rural areas notaries even double up as a form of estate agent, effectively administering all property-related aspects of village life.

But notaries do not act in an advisory capacity or even, in theory at least, serve to protect the interests of their 'clients' – they are agents of the state, albeit ones who work as self-employed businesspeople. So while their role is an important one, it is vital, given the legal issues outlined above, for foreign buyers not to see them as a substitute for independent legal advice.

Notaries' fees are fixed by governments, on a sliding scale according to the value of the property. Expect to pay between 1 and 2% of the purchase price for the handling of a simple title transfer. If extra work is involved, for example to establish clear title on a very old property, the total fee may be more like 5-6%.

If you and the seller each have a separate notary, by convention they will split the fee between them – so it costs nothing extra to take this approach.

Agreeing to buy

In most places you are likely to be thinking about buying, you will need to agree a preliminary contract with the seller as soon as you have decided you want to buy the property. This differs from the UK, where buyers are not formally committed until much later in proceedings.

It is worth noting that in most countries you have the option of making a formal written offer once you have indicated that you want to buy the property. Such offers are legally binding, and simply state that you wish to buy the stated property for a stated price, and will complete the transaction within a stated period. You would normally be expected to pay a deposit at this point – perhaps up to 5% of the price offered – although if your lawyer words the offer correctly this money may be refundable in certain, defined circumstances.

Making an offer in this way commits you to buy, but does nothing to secure an equivalent commitment from the seller, and most lawyers advise that such an approach is best avoided if at all possible.

The more common, and more even-handed, approach is to move straight to a binding, bilateral agreement – a preliminary contract that commits both parties to the transaction. As a precursor to this you will have had to negotiate verbally, usually via the estate agent, if you wanted a reduction in the advertised purchase price (see page 74).

THE PRELIMINARY CONTRACT

At its simplest, the preliminary contract says that the seller must sell the stated property at an agreed price, on a fixed date, to the buyer; and that the buyer must buy it; and that if for some reason either party fails to complete the transaction, the other one can force them, through the courts, to do so.

The key to arriving at a good preliminary contract, though, is to negotiate a series of 'get out' clauses which protect you from having to complete the deal in the event of anything arising that could put you off

 Remember that the preliminary contract is a private deal between you and the seller. Never sign one or hand over any money before showing it to an independent lawyer. See pages 76-8.

wanting to buy, or prevent you from doing so.

Depending on how quickly you and/or the seller want to seal the deal, you may need to sign the preliminary contract before key elements of the paperwork relating to the sale have been sorted out – before searches have been done, before your mortgage application has been agreed and before it is clear that the property may be eligible for a future planning permission application, for example. Working closely with your lawyer, you should try to negotiate a contract that makes provision for you to walk away if such issues give rise to problems.

In theory it is possible to include any number of get-out clauses in the preliminary contract, but it is important to appreciate that everything inserted must be agreed by both parties, so the clauses must not appear too onerous from the seller's perspective. The seller is unlikely to agree to a clause about you needing to sell another property in order to raise the finance for the purchase, for example, because this has obvious potential to scupper the whole deal and at the very least could delay the signing of the final deed.

In consultation with your lawyer you will need to decide which clauses are non-negotiable from your point of view, and in some cases this may mean delaying signing the contract – for example if you are insistent on having the results of a full structural survey before you commit.

The wording of get-out clauses can be all-important, and it is here that your lawyer's skill will come into its own.

You might negotiate a get-out clause saying simply that the purchase is dependent on you raising mortgage finance, for example – which may sound reasonable. But if the clause said only that, the seller would be within their rights to insist that you take any mortgage – regardless of how punitive the interest rate – in order to

❝Try to negotiate a contract that makes provision for you to walk away from the deal. ❞

complete the transaction. If instead your lawyer manages to negotiate a clause saying the purchase is subject to you securing a loan at less than a defined rate of interest, you are much better protected.

Get-out clauses

These are a crucial part of the negotiation and allow you to pull out if things go wrong. They safeguard your rights as a buyer and prevent you from being compelled to complete the purchase against your will. Professional legal advice is essential here.

Standard clauses in a preliminary contract would address the following:

- Names, addresses and identifying details of the buyer and seller, along with details of your 'civil state'.
- Full description of the property, and relevant land registry details.
- Details of exactly what is included in, and excluded from, the sale.
- Statement that the property is sold subject to any rights that exist over it, but that the seller him- or herself has not created any.
- Statement that the property is sold with vacant possession.

What is your 'civil state'?

Your 'civil state' is a concept much more familiar in continental Europe than in the UK, and forms part of the deed of sale in property transactions.

Basically it is a comprehensive set of information about you including, as well as your name and address, your occupation, nationality, passport number, maiden name, the names of your parents, your date and place of birth, date and place of marriage and 'matrimonial regime'.

The authorities are entitled to ask for proof of all the points in your 'civil state', in the form of birth and marriage certificates, for example; they may also require official Spanish translations. It is worth asking your lawyer what documents will be required and when, or you could discover at the final signing ceremony that you are unwittingly in breach of contract.

- Details of the deposit being paid.
- Details of what will happen if the contract is broken.
- Name of the notary who will prepare the final deed of sale.
- Statement that full details of title will be included in the final deed of sale.
- Date for signing of the final deed of sale.
- Statement about when the buyer will take possession of the property.
- The price to be paid.
- Statement about who will pay the costs of the purchase.
- Details of the estate agent and who will pay their commission.

Typical get-out clauses would cover the following:

- That in legal terms, the property and its boundaries match what you think you are buying.
- That the seller is actually the owner of the property, and is entitled to sell it.
- That if there are any debts or mortgages secured against the property, these will be paid by the seller before legal ownership transfers to you.
- That the proper planning consents have been secured for work done at the property, building regulations have been followed, and any related fines paid.
- That any land bought for development is properly designated as land permitted to be developed.

- Issues relating to rights of way and pre-emption rights.
- Issues relating to stage payments, completion dates, bank guarantees and building licenses if buying off-plan.

Note that in some countries – normally non-EU countries or ones that have recently joined – you will need to gain approval from the government to buy property. To apply, you will need to supply a copy of the preliminary contract, along with proof of income and identification information; there will be a small fee to pay. Applications are normally granted with no difficulty, but you may want to take legal advice locally about what would happen if it was not forthcoming. For further information on this aspect of buying in particular countries, see Chapter 8.

66 In some countries you will need to gain approval from the government to buy property. 99

Buying in Florida

Like many of their European counterparts, Floridians generally buy and sell homes without involving a lawyer. But instead of relying on notaries to handle transactions, they use 'title insurance companies' to conduct the conveyancing.

Such firms examine the public records to make sure the seller owns the property, and on the basis of these searches insure the property against a third party making a claim against it.

As a foreigner it is best to engage a lawyer to handle the purchase, because you can ask them to draft and manage a purchase contract at the same time. Make sure they are registered title insurance agents; otherwise they will have to sub-contract to a title insurance firm at extra cost.

Given that the language barrier is less of an issue in the US, you may be more confident about engaging the services of a locally qualified lawyer, rather than one based in the UK.

As in Europe, preliminary contracts are the key documents in any Floridian house transaction, with the same emphasis on negotiation of get-out clauses to protect your interests.

The only other significant difference when buying in Florida is that you will pay your deposit to an 'escrow agent', usually selected by your estate agent but subject to approval of all parties. He or she is responsible for checking all documents and ensuring the transaction 'closes' within the period specified in the preliminary contract.

BUYING AN UNFINISHED PROPERTY

When the transaction involves a property that has yet to be built, or is not yet finished, you will generally be asked to sign a reservation contract, whereby you agree to buy the property once it has been built, and agree to make payments in stages as the construction progresses.

" Ask your lawyer to hold out for a French-style payment schedule. "

In France there are rules about how big a deposit the developer can ask for at this point and about how staged payments should be handled (see box, right), but in most other countries developers push to get away with demanding staged payments on set dates, regardless of progress – or lack of it – on site. It is well worth asking your lawyer to hold out for a French-style payment schedule.

Generally speaking the reservation contract should include:

- A full description of the property to be built, its size and number of rooms.
- Details of shared facilities or services to be provided.
- Details of the price and any ways in which this might vary, for example to pay for extra facilities.

- Details of the reservation fee and staged payments schedule, and about where such money will be kept until legal title is transferred.
- A specification of the circumstances in which the reservation fee is to be repaid, for example if the final deed of sale is not signed on the agreed date because the developer has defaulted; if the price is more than a certain percentage above the initial price; if mortgage finance at a suitable rate of interest cannot be secured; or if the property is smaller or of reduced quality.
- Provision for the buyer to receive a draft title deed at least a month before the signing date.
- Details about developers' guarantees.
- Provision that transfer of legal title will take place when the developer becomes the legal owner of the property and is able to offer you a legal guarantee that either the construction of the property will be completed or that if it is not, your funds will be repaid.

The developer's guarantee

The developer's guarantee is a crucial part of any off-plan purchase, and is a legal requirement in many countries; although in some areas developers do still try to get away without giving one.

There are two types of guarantee – so-called 'extrinsic' guarantees, whereby the developer has persuaded a bank to accept joint liability and complete the building if the developer fails to do so; and 'intrinsic' ones, whereby the developer just promises to pay you back the money you have already spent on the property if it is unable to meet its obligations. Clearly the former type is preferable, but few developers will state in advance that a bank guarantee will definitely be in place.

Bear in mind that when buying off-plan you should also have copies of:

- A full specification for the property (check this carefully because it has been known for developers to produce a fantastically well equipped show apartment, but specify much poorer quality fixtures and fittings for some or all of the rest of the development).
- A copy of the community rules and constitution.
- Information about any arrangements for management or letting of the property.
- Planning permission/building licenses.

❝ The developer's guarantee is a crucial part of any off-plan purchase. ❞

Jargon buster

Developers' guarantees
There are two types of developer's guarantee:

'extrinsic' where a bank has accepted joint liability with the developer and will be responsible for completing the building if the developer fails to do so (if it goes bankrupt, for example). This is now mandatory in Italy.

'intrinsic' a less comprehensive guarantee whereby the developer simply promises to pay back the money you have already spent on the property if it is unable to meet its obligations.

Staged payments in France

When buying off-plan you will pay:

A 5% deposit on signing of the *contrat de reservation* (or 2% if the completion date is more than a year away)

A further 30% (or 33%) on completion of the foundations of the property.

A further 35% when the property is weatherproof.

A further 25% on completion of the construction of the property.

The remaining 5% when you receive the keys (although you may withhold this if you feel the developer has not complied with the property specifications).

Using building professionals

Especially if you are buying a rundown property for renovation, or are buying a plot to build on, you are likely to want to talk to a variety of building professionals to make sure what you want to do can be achieved, and at a reasonable cost.

SURVEYORS

There is less of a tradition of pre-purchase property surveys in continental Europe than there is in the UK, and some sellers may look at you as if you have suddenly sprouted a second head if you suggest that you want a surveyor to prod around their precious soon-to-be-former home. Many will refuse to have a 'subject to survey' clause inserted into the preliminary contract, so if you want a survey done, you may need to move fast or you may risk losing the sale.

If you are buying an old property it is well worth insisting on having a proper survey done, though, to reassure yourself that the place is not about to collapse, and to get some idea of how much work is needed to bring the property up to modern

> **❝ If you are buying an old property it is well worth insisting on having a proper survey done. ❞**

standards. Back home if you commission a survey and it highlights a problem with the property it is often considered reasonable to ask for some money off the price; whether or not you decide to opt for this approach, and what the seller's reaction will be, depends entirely on the circumstances.

In most areas where there is a tradition of British and other north European second home buyers it is possible to find British-qualified chartered surveyors. You may find one through personal recommendation, through the local equivalent of Yellow Pages, or through the Royal Institution

---

! Builder's estimate

A less formal alternative to having a property inspected by a surveyor is to have a builder estimate the cost of repairs and restoration. This may be useful but remember that an estimate is not binding and the eventual cost could be considerably higher.

of Chartered Surveyors, which has offices in Austria, Belgium/ Luxembourg, Cyprus, Czech Republic, Denmark, France, Germany, Greece, Hungary, Italy, Malta, Netherlands, Poland, Portugal, Spain and Switzerland. You can find contact details via the RICS Worldwide homepage – follow the link from www.rics.org.uk.

If what you want is a basic survey providing information on the general state of repair and condition of the property – and some idea of its value – ask for a home buyer's report, which should cost you a minimum of around £300.

A more detailed structural survey – whereby the surveyor will examine the condition of the building looking for signs of cracking, movement, deterioration, rot and damp; inspect services like gas, electricity and water where possible; outline defects and where possible suggest solutions and likely costs – may cost you upwards of £1,000.

Some surveyors will also undertake off-plan construction progress reports to keep you up to date with how your developer is performing; and 'snagging' surveys to report differences between what an off-plan property should be like, and its condition at hand-over.

Depending on where you are buying, there are other professionals you may employ to do the same kind of surveys. In France you might engage the services of an *expert*

Checklist of issues you may ask the surveyor to cover

- Adequacy of foundations
- Roof/beams
- Cement quality (where the building is constructed out of cement)
- Heating and air conditioning
- Drains, up to the point where they meet the main sewer or septic tank
- Septic tank check
- Electrics
- Rot
- Wood-boring insects
- Asbestos
- Swimming pool and related equipment

---

immobilier, for example, who can produce either an *expertise* (similar to the home buyer's report) or a *bilan de sante* (more like a full structural survey). In Italy a *geometra* (see page 83) should provide a similar service, as well as being able to project manage any renovation work required at the property.

Jargon buster

Surveyors
expert immobilier French surveyor. Do not confuse with an agent immobilier, who is an estate agent
agrimensor Spanish surveyor
geometra Italian surveyor
home inspector American surveyor, used in Florida

More detailed surveys and inspections, for example to look for insect infestations, can be commissioned from all these professionals and will cost extra, but could save you a lot of money in the long run.

To find an expert immobilier, search by location on the online database of the Chambre des Experts Immobiliers, whose website is at www.experts-fnaim.org.

If you are buying in Florida, you will need to employ a 'home inspector', and in many areas it is sensible to have him or her look particularly for evidence of termites and other wood-boring insects, which are fairly common. Look for an inspector who is a member of the American Society of Home Inspectors, whose website is at www.ashi.com.

ARCHITECTS

For major building work requiring an architect, you are likely to want to employ someone local, which may mean asking around for recommendations or looking around for properties that you feel have been built or 'done up' successfully and enquiring about who was in charge of the project.

If you are having a survey done, you may want to ask the surveyor for some names of architects you might use; although in some cases architects can conduct surveys themselves.

If you have never used an architect before, you may find it useful to talk to the Royal Institute of British Architects, both to get an idea of how best to make use of the services of an architect, and to get help finding one. The organisation has an online database of more than 4,000 registered practices, including some based outside the UK.

The Architects' Council of Europe represents around 450,000 architects in the 25 EU member states, plus Switzerland, Norway, Bulgaria, Croatia, Romania and Turkey. The website lists contact details for architects' representative bodies in each country, which should be able to offer guidance on finding a reputable architect. In some cases these national bodies list UK-qualified architects operating in the country, as well as local architects.

BUILDERS

If you are building from scratch – which may, in many places, be cheaper than restoring a ruin – you may be planning to engage a large building company, which is likely to have 'off the shelf' designs for various types of home, perhaps as part of deal

To contact the Royal Institute of British Architects (RIBA) visit their website at www.architecture.com. To contact the Architects' Council of Europe, go to www.ace-cae.org

whereby you buy a plot of land on a villa complex where a large building company/developer then builds individual houses to buyers' requirements.

Whether you go down this or the architect route, your first priority must be to ask your lawyer to investigate the proposed land plot thoroughly, including examining the title of the land and checking out its planning status. If you are buying a plot on an existing estate, as many people do, you should have no problems getting a building permit, but it is vital to check before signing a preliminary contract for the land and thus committing to the purchase.

Check also that the purchase price of any land you are planning to buy includes all services – water, paved road, electricity and sewage – up to the boundary of your plot. If you are buying on a deal whereby the seller is a builder or developer who could construct the property for you, make sure your contract allows you to get rid of them and bring in other builders.

Once your lawyer gives you the go-ahead to buy the land, on the basis that there is no reason why you should not be able to obtain a building permit, you will need to commission a set of plans and detailed specifications for the building and – if you are appointing your own builder – get detailed quotations from if possible, at least three builders. This may not always be easy, because

" Building from scratch may, in many places, turn out be cheaper than trying to restore a total ruin. "

builders in many parts of Europe are extremely busy, but unless you get some comparative quotes you will never know whether you have paid over the odds for the work.

Once you have chosen a builder, you will need to negotiate a contract with them, which could be done via an exchange of signed letters including details of the work to be carried out, the price, the agreed start date and contract duration. You should insert a penalty clause for late completion, which means that if the work is not completed on time the builder must pay you damages. You should also agree on stage payments, which could be paid monthly or quarterly, or be linked to completion of certain elements of the work. Insist on written quotations and invoices, and only pay for work when you are happy with it.

Penalty clauses

If you agree these in writing with your builder he will be under financial pressure to complete the work on time. Many builders will resist them, however.

Money matters

Even if you have chosen a property that is going for a song, the buying process requires you to hand over large sums of money at different stages, so it is important to be prepared and have your finances properly organised.

DEPOSITS

The paying of deposits when buying property is largely a matter of custom, but regardless of this you may in fact want to volunteer a small goodwill deposit as a gesture if there is likely to be a delay before signing the preliminary contract (if you want to conduct a survey and/or make enquiries about planning issues, for example). A small deposit may be just the sweetener needed to persuade the seller to keep the property off the market while you straighten out a few essentials before signing on the dotted line.

At the point of signing the preliminary contract, you will generally be expected to hand over a substantial sum – which may range from 10% to a third of the purchase price, depending on what and where you are buying. If you make a formal offer to buy, rather than going straight to a preliminary contract, you would normally be expected to pay a deposit of up to 5% of the purchase price.

What happens in the case of either party defaulting on the contract depends, again, on local custom and the way your lawyer handles the handing over of the deposit (see box).

Deposit levels are often more negotiable than one might think, but although it can be tempting to push for as low a deposit as possible, bear in mind that if you only pay a low deposit, the seller may end up better off defaulting on their contract with you and paying you back twice the

---

Agents demanding early deposits

Some estate agents insist that potential buyers be prepared to pay a deposit the moment they see a property they like - sometimes even suggesting that they should leave the UK clutching a banker's draft for a set amount to be put down against a property.

The best advice is to refuse. Deposits, if they are to have any real purpose, must be non-refundable - and should only, therefore, be requested when both parties to the transaction are ready to commit to the deal.

Take your time and have your lawyer negotiate a contract you are happy with, before arranging for the money to be sent by electronic transfer to their account.

---

deposit amount, if another buyer comes along with a significantly better offer.

Never hand over deposit money directly to the seller, or even to the estate agent – unless they are fully bonded. In most cases the safest approach is to lodge monies either with your own lawyer, or with the notary handling the sale.

PAYING THE BALANCE

Whatever deposit you have paid, the remainder of the money will come due when you sign the formal deed of sale, so if you are paying in cash or remortgaging your UK home you will need to have the money, exchanged into the local currency, ready to be paid into the notary's account for this time. If the bulk of the purchase is being funded from an overseas mortgage, you will need to ensure the lender is ready to release the money in readiness for the final signing.

The only exception to this is if you are buying off-plan, in which case money will be due in stages through the building process – so if you are borrowing to fund the purchase you will need to negotiate with your lender for them to allow you to draw down the mortgage in stages. This may seem like extra hassle, but it does have the advantage that in the run-up to taking possession of the property your monthly repayments will increase gradually, as you should only be paying interest on the portion of the loan that has been released.

What happens if I pull out?

In most cases, deposits are non-refundable other than in defined situations as laid out in the preliminary contract; the whole point of them is that they help tie you in to buying the property, because you know that if you were to walk away you would lose your money.

So if all goes well, your deposit will sit in a special bank account at your lawyer's office, until the signing of the preliminary contract, at which point it will be released to the seller in part-payment for the property.

If you default on the contract, other than in the permitted ways agreed in the preliminary contract, the deposit money will remain with the seller by way of compensation. In most cases the seller would also have the right to sue you for any damages resulting from the breach of contract. If the seller defaults, you are normally entitled to twice the amount of the deposit in compensation.

Your lawyer must ensure that the wording of the contract makes clear how the deposit is being offered. In Italy, for example, there is a distinction between a *caparra confirmatoria* - whereby you and the seller retain the right to force the sale through the courts in case of default; and a *caparra penitenziale* - whereby this right of redress is forfeited.

OTHER COSTS

Property transfer taxes – wherever you buy, you will be liable for taxes relating to the transfer of the property into your ownership, including land registration fees and stamp duty, which altogether could cost up to 10% of the purchase price; or even more if you are buying somewhere registered as 'rural'.

VAT – this is chargeable on new properties, and depending on what and where you are buying, and whether it will be your primary residence, could cost you anything from 10-20% of the purchase price. Buying in certain ways, including through a leaseback scheme, can exempt you from VAT.

Legal costs – again, these vary according to where and what you are buying, and what particular services you have asked your lawyer and notary to perform. Generally speaking it is worth setting aside 3-4% of the purchase price in total to cover these.

Estate agents' fees – highly variable, but generally allow between 2-6% of the purchase price to cover your part of the fees. In the UK only the seller pays an agent, but in other countries the cost is often split between both parties. See page 153 for more details.

BUYING YOUR MONEY

Wherever you are buying, you will need to arrange for your UK money to be exchanged into the local currency, whether that be dollars, euros or any other denomination. You could be exchanging an awful lot of money by the time the purchase is complete, so it makes sense to hunt around for the best possible deal.

Currency risk can affect your buying power enormously, so it is vital to make sure your money is working as hard as it possibly can. You may want to negotiate forward deals with specialist currency brokers, if you think the exchange rate is heading in an unfavourable direction (see page 35). Otherwise, shop around for the best rate. Your UK bank should offer you a rate considerably better than the tourist rate advertised in branches; and specialist brokers will almost certainly beat that.

If you are using a UK-based lawyer who deals with a lot of overseas property transactions, they may have preferential deals with banks or brokers that could save you considerable sums.

 Levels of taxation vary considerably, depending on where you are buying. For details of fees and taxes in specific countries see Chapter 8.

Completing the purchase

While the preliminary contract is a private contract between buyer and seller, the final sales deed is what turns that private contract into an official, public transfer of property. It is an important document and you need to check it is accurate and complete.

Depending on how far advanced you are at the point of signing the preliminary contract, your lawyer is likely to have a number of searches and enquiries to make in the period between the ink drying on the initial agreement, and the signing of the final sales deed (see the section below).

Your lawyer, *geometra* or estate agent may have conducted some of these in advance of you signing the preliminary contract; your lawyer should have dealt with any remaining ones through get-out clauses.

THE FINAL SALES DEED

The final sales deed is largely a repeat of the preliminary contract, but with some additional elements. A typical deed would include the following:

- Name and address of the notary.
- Identification of the parties (including details of their civil state – see page 90), and details of anyone with power of attorney (see page 104).
- Full description of the property and any restrictions affecting it.
- Statement about the current claim to ownership of the property, whether or not it is free of tenants, and liability for bills up to the date of completion.
- Price and methods of payment.
- Statement about the taxes payable for the sale, including capital gains tax from the vendor and other duties.
- Confirmation that the sale has taken place.
- Details about the property's planning status.
- Confirmation that anyone with pre-emption rights has renounced them, listing names and addresses where appropriate.
- History of how the vendor came to own the property, along with details of the penultimate owner.

How you declare your 'matrimonial regime' in the deed of sale may have long-term financial implications, particularly in France. See pages 79-80 for further details.

- Date on which the buyer becomes owner, and confirmation of vacant possession.
- Details of any charges against the property, with the sellers' warranties and guarantees that these have been cleared.
- Details of any mortgage finance used to buy the property that has been used to finance the purchase (no details will be given if you are buying through a UK re-mortgage).
- Statement of sincerity, making clear that all statements in the deed are true, the price has been fully stated and that the notary has warned the parties of the sanctions that may flow from false declaration of price.

" You could be putting yourself in a very dangerous position by agreeing to under-declare. "

DECLARING THE PROPERTY PRICE IN THE FINAL DEED

In many parts of continental Europe there is a tradition of under-declaration of property prices in final sales deeds – a form of tax evasion that has been, and continues to be, commonplace in some areas.

The point here is that all the taxes to which one becomes liable when one buys and sells property are based on the value of the property as declared in the deed, rather than necessarily the price actually being paid. In some cases the difference between what the seller would like to declare and the real price is substantial.

Clearly it might be argued that as the buyer of the property you too would gain from under-declaring the value, since property transfer taxes, notary fees and the like are all calculated from the basis of the declared value. But the truth is that the only real winner from under-declaration is the seller, who may stand to gain substantially from a greatly reduced capital gains tax liability.

You could be putting yourself in a very dangerous position by agreeing to under-declare. The authorities are coming down much harder on under-declaration than in the past, and have the right to demand any taxes not paid, along with interest charges and a fine; if there is a clear and intentional under-declaration, they have the right to buy the property back at the price declared, within six months of the transaction going through. This would not only leave you without the home you have just spent several months purchasing, but would leave you substantially out of pocket.

Even if you were to under-declare and escape detection, remember that you would face the same issue if and when you came to sell – and if your buyer were to insist on declaring the true market value at that point, the capital gain on which you were taxed would be disproportionately high.

SEARCHES TO BE DONE BEFORE COMPLETION

Your lawyer should verify the following points before you sign the final sales deed. Failure to do so could cost you dear.

1. A check that the property legally exists and is as described; and that the boundaries of the property as described match those in official land registry records.

2. A check that the seller is the registered owner of the property, and that he or she is selling it free of mortgages.

3. A check on the planning situation of the property, examining what kind of development is possible, subject to suitable planning permission being granted, at the property.

4. A check that the property meets all relevant planning and building regulations, and has all relevant certification (for example a document stating that the property is fit for human habitation).

5. That all relevant housing-related legislation has been complied with, for example that inspections relating to asbestos and wood-boring insects like termites have been conducted.

6. A check that the seller has complied with all relevant tax legislation; if not the property may be unsaleable unless the taxes due, plus fines, are paid.

7. Where the seller is self-employed or a company, that they have not been declared bankrupt or gone into liquidation, and there are no such applications pending.

8. A check to show that all relevant service charges, ground rents and the like have been paid.

9. A check to ensure that all relevant pre-emption rights have been attended to in the proper manner. These might include neighbours' rights to first refusal to buy land if in a rural area, and other authorities' rights to buy, for example if a road-widening scheme is happening nearby.

10. A check that all outstanding mortgages and other debts secured against the property have been cleared (if not, these debts remain with the property and would become your responsibility).

POWER OF ATTORNEY

This is a legal process that allows a lawyer or notary to act on your behalf where necessary.

In theory, you should be present to sign the final deed of sale, which will take place in the notary's offices. The date of the signing ceremony will have been set in the preliminary contract – normally around two months after the preliminary contract is signed – but as is often the case with legal matters, the completion date may end up having to change because of unforeseen delays.

These delays may result from issues like particular search documents not having arrived or money being temporarily stuck in the banking system. It should normally be possible to know a definite signing date a week or two beforehand, but this may not always be the case.

If you were buying in the UK such delays would probably be less of a problem, but when buying abroad they can prove extremely inconvenient. To be sure of getting there at a reasonable cost requires certainty about dates in order to book flights and accommodation, and it is not always possible to drop everything at home and rearrange flights to fit in with a change in timing.

Because of this, and because there may be aspects of the buying process that require a speedy signature from you, it is usually sensible to take the precaution of signing over power of attorney to your lawyer, notary or a notary's clerk.

The power of attorney document authorises them to do specific things on your behalf, and must be very specific. So for example if you want your lawyer to be able to sign the title deed and draw a cheque on a bank account you have set up in the country in which you are buying, the document will need to grant authorisation for both activities. It will also need to give a description of the property, the price agreed and the method of payment to be used.

Setting up a power of attorney can only be done in front of a notary; there are different ways of setting it up and your lawyer should be able to advise you on this. One approach is to set the power up in front of a notary at home and then have this approved by the Foreign and Commonwealth Office for use abroad.

Clearly granting power of attorney is something you should only ever do to someone who has your complete trust; it should also be time-limited, so you may want to set one up for, say, a six month period.

The tax authorities recognise that the long history of under-declaration can make capital gains tax liability for sellers a major headache, so they can normally be relied upon to turn a blind eye to relatively small under-declarations. But sellers should set their asking price at a level that enables them to clear all their tax liabilities, so the most legally and financially sensible approach is to insist on full declaration.

FINAL STEPS BEFORE COMPLETION

In the weeks before completion of the transaction, there are several issues you should be focusing on with your lawyer:

- Sort out power of attorney (see box).
- Check what documents you need to produce on signing the final deed.
- Confirm that all the conditions built into the preliminary contract have been complied with.
- Confirm that all other enquiries and concerns have been dealt with, for example that you have received any condominium rules.
- Confirm that the seller has paid all relevant fees, taxes and other bills.
- Confirm that a draft of the final deed has been received – if possible

a month before the signing date.

- Check that, if appropriate, the seller has applied for, and been granted, exemption from capital gains tax.
- Confirm arrangements for completion with the notary and pass these on to your mortgage lender, including date, time and place for money to be released.
- Send necessary funds to your lawyer.
- Sign off pre-purchase snags if you are buying off-plan.

POST-SIGNING PROCEDURES

After the deed is signed, the notary will take, from the money you have sent, the taxes you owe to the state and his or her fees. From the balance he or she will then pay off any money due to the estate agent and, if relevant, the condominium; pay off any remaining debts secured against the property; and then give the remainder of the balance to the seller.

Your title to the property, and any mortgage, must then be registered at the land registry; there is a legal time limit within which this must be done, but your lawyer should push for it to be done as soon as possible, because there is a (hopefully only hypothetical) danger of someone else registering

Before completion you will need to have set up a local bank account and obtained a tax number. See page 109 and Chapter 8 for further details.

Capital gains taxes in Spain

In Spain, there is a local capital gains tax called plus valia, which is levied on property sellers.

By convention this is paid by the buyer, because the bill for the tax normally arrives after the sale has gone through and the liability stays with the property rather than the previous owner. In most cases the amount in question is fairly small, but if the property has not been sold for a long while and the value has shot up, it can be substantial.

It is advisable to ask your lawyer to contact the local town hall to find out how much is due, and negotiate for that amount to be deducted from the purchase price - or agree a clause in the preliminary contract that the seller must pay (although bear in mind that the bill will still come to you, and it will be up to you to chase the vendor to fulfil this part of the contract - or take them to court to force them to do so).

As a separate point you must by law hold back 5% of the purchase price and pay this to the tax authorities rather than to the seller, to set against their capital gains tax liability from the sale. This amount will be set against the seller's total tax liability at the point of signing the deed, unless he or she has previously provided proof of exemption from the tax.

another transaction, like a debt or court judgement, against the property. Whoever registers first gets priority, so you could in theory become liable for a debt run up by the previous owner, if this is registered before your title.

After a few months you will receive, via the notary, confirmation that the title has been registered. At this point you will receive a final statement from the notary explaining how your money has been spent. If you are lucky the notary will have slightly over-estimated their costs before the signing, so you will be due a small refund.

Being an owner

Completing the purchase of your property is a big step but it is only the beginning of an on-going process. As the owner of an overseas property you have various responsibilities and duties to attend to and a long list of practical considerations, from repairs and restoration to lettings and tax.

Sorting out the essentials

Once you have signed the final deed, you will be able to relax a little. But your work as an overseas property owner has only just begun, and you will probably have very little time in which to put your feet up at this stage. There are immediate tasks to tackle and long-term issues to consider.

On an immediate level, your priorities will be, if you have not already done so:

- To make sure all the relevant services to the property are connected and properly transferred into your name.
- To set up a bank account through which to pay your bills.
- To insure the property.

ARRANGING UTILITY CONNECTIONS

If you have bought an established property, you will generally just take over the existing electricity supply from the previous owners. You should have been able to set up for a meter reading in advance, so that you are only responsible for bills after the date of completion – if not you will need to do this as soon as possible. You will be charged a small fee for the transfer.

If you are buying a new property,

this will be connected to the electricity supply but you will have to contact your electricity supplier to arrange which tariff you should be on. Depending on where you are buying this may be handled in various ways, but in some places you will need to estimate the peak wattage you need by supplying them with information about the maximum number of appliances likely to be in use at any one time. Try to make sure you do not under-estimate this, especially if other people are going to use the property, because otherwise you may find that the supply cuts out at times of highest demand.

Bear in mind that if you are buying an old property, the wiring may be obsolete, and will need upgrading, at your expense, to modern standards.

If the property is not yet connected to mains electricity or gas (which is often only available in larger towns and cities), the costs of connection

 Although you would generally take over the existing supply from the previous owners, for specific details of utility providers in different countries, see Chapter 8.

can be prohibitive, so make sure you have factored this in to your affordability calculations before committing to buy. In some areas, you may find it considerably cheaper to stick with bottled gas, which you can arrange to be delivered regularly or buy yourself from hardware stores.

Depending on where you have bought, you will also need to contact your water supplier, which may be the local council, to set up or transfer a supply. Again, the costs of establishing a connection can be high so make sure you have thought carefully about this before buying.

The relevant suppliers and/or your surveyor should be able to provide relevant advice and quotes. The easiest way to pay for utilities is to set up direct debits from a local bank account.

OPENING BANK ACCOUNTS

Even if you will only be visiting your property infrequently, you will need a local current account from which to pay bills. The presence of British banks abroad, and local banks catering for an English-speaking clientele, varies considerably depending on demand from expatriates and second home owners.

Charges for transferring money between the UK and overseas also varies according to which UK bank, and which local bank, you use – so it is well worth shopping around to find the best deals and the arrangement that best meets your circumstances.

You should normally encounter no problems setting up a local bank account, other than needing to produce relevant proof of identity, proof of your overseas address and your tax code – or, depending on where you have bought, a residence card; although in some cases you may also be asked for your translated 'civil state' paperwork – all of which you will already have by virtue of going through the property buying process.

Make sure you understand the rules on use of cheques, overdrafts and the like, as these can vary considerably from those in the UK. In France cheques are used much more commonly than is the case in the UK, for example, and if – as most second home owners do – you are opening a 'non-resident' bank account, be aware that it is unlikely to offer an overdraft facility. Even if you have a standard account, going into unauthorised overdraft can be dealt with much more harshly than one might expect. It is well worth keeping your account well stocked with a cash cushion, to avoid unforeseen problems.

ARRANGING INSURANCE

Wherever you are buying, you will need to make sure your property is adequately insured, which means insuring the building itself as well as the contents – although if you are buying an apartment, the buildings insurance should already be included in the service charge.

Make sure the sums insured are sufficient to cover you in case of a total loss, and that the policy is appropriate for your circumstances –

around for a more appropriate policy at the earliest opportunity.

In some parts of the world, extra insurance against hurricane, earthquake or flood damage is advisable, although this can be prohibitively expensive. High risk areas include parts of Florida and some locations in Turkey (see page 186).

“ Make sure the sums insured are sufficient to cover you in case of a total loss. ”

for example, that it covers you for letting the property out, and for periods where the property may be empty.

It may be possible for you to take over the previous owner's insurance policy, and indeed this may happen automatically unless you have specified during the buying process that you want to make your own arrangements. But particularly if you are planning to let the property out you will almost certainly want to shop

 For more information on home insurance overseas and special considerations if you are letting your property out, see pages 122-3.

Renovating your property

If you plan to make major renovations to your newly acquired property, you probably won't want to wait long before getting down to business. Speed is essential if you hope to start earning from lettings, less so if you are simply planning a private holiday home.

PLANNING PERMISSION

As explained in chapter 4, checking out the planning status of your property should have been one of your main priorities in the period before committing to buy the property.

The niceties of gaining planning permission vary between areas, and depend considerably on the size and nature of the project. Generally speaking, the larger the property, the more historically or architecturally unique it is, and the more environmentally special its surrounding area is, the stricter the rules will be; and the longer the planning approval process will take. Planning applications should take at least a couple of months, possibly more; and are best handled by a professional with intimate knowledge of the vagaries of the local system.

Chances are that if your purchase of the property was dependent on being able to renovate it, you will have insisted on waiting for planning approval to come through before completing the deal; and particularly if there is a lot of work to be done, you will already have consulted with architects to produce and submit detailed plans, and get the project off the ground.

If you have not already engaged a building team to do whatever work you have planned, you will need to move quickly in order to maximise your use of the property, and to avoid having to re-apply for planning permission – which is normally time-limited.

ARCHITECTS AND BUILDERS

As explained in Chapter 4, spend time finding an architect and/or builder you feel you can trust to do the work properly. Before you agree a contract for the work to begin, check the following:

- That they have the necessary qualifications and are registered as traders with the relevant chamber of commerce.
- Where appropriate, that they have a bond which gives you a guarantee of workmanship for a set period.

111

- That they have third party insurance which provides cover in case they accidentally cause damage to the house during the renovation.
- That you have insurance to cover you if they have an accident on your property, or produce faulty workmanship. You may be able to add this to a standard buildings insurance policy, at extra cost.

❝Your architect may be held responsible for mistaken instructions to the builder and for problems with the land... such as subsidence.❞

Check with your lawyer how you stand legally in terms of guarantees, and come-back in case problems arise; for example your architect may be held responsible for mistaken instructions to the builder and for problems with the land that he or she has not detected, such as subsidence.

Project managing a property renovation at a distance can be a considerable challenge, and many buyers who do not have the luxury of taking huge chunks of time off to be on site find life easier if they appoint an architect, *geometra* or similar building professional to manage the project on their behalf.

In most areas finding a specialist firm to undertake this kind of work should be relatively straightforward, either by asking other UK owners for recommendations or by contacting firms via the local Yellow Pages or professional bodies. Some rental management companies will also provide such services.

Make sure you are happy with all aspects of the arrangement though, because the cost of project management can be high and renovation costs have the potential to spiral out of control if the project manager takes their eye off the ball.

If you experience problems with bad service from a building professional overseas, first try to resolve it with them directly. If this does not work, you may have recourse to the relevant professional association or chamber of commerce, or to your insurer. If all else fails, you may want to contact a local lawyer – perhaps the one you bought the property through – to see if they can help. Be warned that taking any of the building professions to court can be a long, painful and expensive process, however.

Although it normally specialises in problems relating to holidays and goods bought while visiting Europe, the Citizen's Advice Bureau European Consumer Centre may also be able to offer advice. Write to the UK European Consumer Centre, PO Box 3308, Wolverhampton WV10 9ZS or email: euroconsumer@citizensadvice.org.uk.

APPOINTING A PROJECT MANAGER

Project managing at a distance is a challenging process. Most people find it easier to appoint a professional to manage the project on their behalf.

The cost of having a firm managing the architectural design, material specification and sourcing, and securing planning and other approvals could be around 5% of the overall conversion cost. Project management could cost a further 10%, and you will also need to factor in additional costs for landscaping.

Issues to think about when choosing a project manager include:

1. Their English and native language skills

2. Their qualifications and whether they are members of relevant professional associations

3. Evidence of their skills, from previous projects – ask for testimonials from previous English-speaking clients if at all possible

4. The procedures they plan to follow in terms of keeping you updated on progress (do they offer to provide regular email updates, including photos, for example?)

5. The estimated cost and scheme for payments

6. The estimated completion date.

Maintaining your property

Whichever way you plan to use your property, you have just taken on a big maintenance commitment. Upkeep presents particular problems if you are living a long way from your property and are not in a position to visit it regularly. Holiday lets can be demanding.

Think about how much work is involved in maintaining your UK home – how much time and money you spend looking after it, replacing appliances and furniture, fixing things or paying people to mend them when they go wrong. Throw distance into the mix and it is easy to see that looking after another property hundreds of miles away could take plenty of organising, and an awful lot of money.

&& Remember that maintenance and repair costs can be offset against your tax liabilities. %%

DOING IT YOURSELF

If you own your new property on a freehold basis, you are responsible for all the maintenance and repair yourself and will need as much as possible to budget for unforeseen costs, like the boiler breaking down and needing replacing, or a loose roof

tile causing flood damage to the upstairs ceilings.

Depending on your policy, you may be able to claim for some sorts of problems through your buildings insurance, but most everyday costs – and the costs of preventative work that can prevent bigger problems happening in the future, like clearing leaves and other debris out of the drains and gutters in order to prevent flooding, will be down to you.

You may find it useful to save extra money into the overseas bank account through which you pay your utility bills, to help cover such expenses when they arise.

If you have bought in an apartment or condominium-style development, you can expect the majority of day to day maintenance problems relating to the buildings and facilities beyond the boundaries of your property to be paid for out of your service charge. But watch out for big expenditures which could hit the whole community, like a replacement roof. You will only be responsible for your 'share' of these costs, but they may be substantial – and you have little or no choice over whether and when they need to be done.

Your lawyer should have checked what maintenance work the company in charge of the development has done in the past, and details of any planned works, before you bought – so this should give you some idea at least of what costs you are likely to incur in future years.

The costs of furnishing your property and dealing with internal maintenance and repairs will be your responsibility, and these can take on particular significance if you are buying as an investment and will be dependent on rental income.

Depending on how upmarket are the tenants you hope to attract, you are likely to have to spend a minimum of several thousands of pounds furnishing and decorating a small to medium sized buy-to-let property from scratch for occupation by tenants, and will need to spend hundreds more every year making sure it remains clean and with everything in working order.

This money will hopefully be well-spent if it keeps your tenants happy enough to continue paying you rent – which, if the property is not beyond your budget and you prepared your finances properly in advance of buying, should be enough to cover the

Being an owner

Where's the kitchen?

An issue to bear in mind when buying in much of Europe is that kitchens are often not included in the initial purchase price of new properties, as they are considered more akin to furniture than is the case in the UK. Off-plan apartments will frequently be offered for sale without a kitchen, although the developer may offer you a choice of fitted kitchen options at extra cost.

Even if you buy a second-hand property, you may find that there was a kitchen there when you viewed it but the owner took it away with them by the time you took possession – hopefully this will have not come as a shock to you, as the detail of what was and was not included in the sale should have been clarified in the preliminary contract.

ongoing expenses, even if not the upfront costs. Remember also that maintenance and repair costs can be offset against your tax liabilities, further details of which are available on pages 128-32.

Bear in mind that with a bit of luck, taking a long-term view on maintenance and repairs could pay dividends by raising the overall value of the property too – so for example,

 In the process of buying the property, your lawyer should have investigated the service charges, guarantees and condominium rules. See page 85.

there may come a point where you would be better to invest in a whole new bathroom than to re-grout the existing one for the umpteenth time. It may cost you a few thousand pounds upfront to have done, but it could add

> **" Insist on seeing properties that the management company manages for absent owners. "**

£10,000 to the value of the property. And if you do not have the financial freedom to make such trade-offs, you should perhaps question whether you have enough money to afford a second home in the first place!

LEASEBACK SCHEMES
One of the big attractions of leaseback schemes is that they take away the headache of dealing with day to day maintenance issues, because all this is handled on your behalf by the management company which runs the development.

The firm will usually sell you a furniture pack as part of the overall purchase deal, which may make life easier for you as an investor but is unlikely to be of the highest quality. It will then be responsible for the

upkeep and general maintenance of the property and will normally pay all the utility bills – although this does depend on the contract you have with the management company.

You may be responsible for a portion of the shared facilities costs depending on the amount of weeks that you use the property, though – and for any building or repair costs that fall outside the guarantees of the builder beyond certain limits set down in your contract.

As with all other aspects of leaseback arrangements, make sure your lawyer has checked the contract carefully so you are aware of what bills might come your way.

APPOINTING A PROPERTY MANAGEMENT FIRM
In the UK, landlords often find it more economical to do their own maintenance and repairs – but this is only possible if the second home is nearby, or if they own a large portfolio of properties and effectively travel around doing maintenance work on them as a full or part-time job.

Even if you are very good at do-it-yourself, plan to do your own maintenance and repair work wherever possible and visit frequently, you will need someone to keep an eye on the property, to let you know if

 If you want further information on leaseback schemes and how they work, see page 17.

some sort of disaster befalls it while you are not around.

You may have friends in the area or have a good relationship with your tenants and/or neighbours and be able to rely on them to perform this function. If not, you will have to pay someone to do it.

Either way, you will almost certainly need on occasion to arrange for trades people to come and fix things at the property – which is not always easy if you are not fluent in the language and have to arrange everything from the UK. Even if you can make yourself understood, it may not be convenient for friends or neighbours to be around to let trades people in, hang around while they do the job and then lock up after them.

All in all, you may find it easier to set up a contract with a property management firm to oversee the place on your behalf.

If you have bought in an area heavily populated with holiday or investment homes, there may be no shortage of companies in your area offering to provide such a service. Your own estate agent may be one of them – but do not just assume that a competent estate agent is also likely to be an effective property manager.

Before appointing anyone, ask for recommendations from your lawyer and any other British buyers you have encountered in the area; if you will be letting the property out, ask for advice from other absentee landlords.

Ask for testimonials from any firm you encounter, and look for companies who are used to working for foreign property owners. Insist on seeing properties that the management company currently manages for

Case Study Everybody needs good neighbours

Alan and Jane Fleetwood, from Cardiff, have a cottage in Normandy which they visit five or six times a year and let out to friends and paying guests on an ad hoc basis.

In 2002, a few months after buying the house, their estate agent in France rang up to say he had been contacted by one of their neighbours, about some storm damage.

'It turned out a tree branch had come down and broken one of the upstairs windows. Even though he didn't know us from Adam, a guy who lived down the road had managed to get into the house, block the window temporarily and arrange for someone to fix it.

'He was so nice about it and wouldn't even let us pay at first - he just kept saying we could settle up when we were next out there. We ended up buying him a case of wine and have since become good friends, but it goes to show that around here at least, this supposed hostility towards English holiday home owners is a myth.'

SERVICES PROVIDED BY A PROPERTY MANAGEMENT FIRM

Property management firms are expensive, but essential for absentee owners offering holiday lets. The range of services differs from firm to firm but you should consider the following:

- Key holding
- Regular external property inspection
- Clearance of letterbox and forwarding of mail to UK address
- Organising tariffs and dealing with utility companies
- Liaising with insurers, lawyers and the like
- Sweeping of drives and patios
- Emailed or posted maintenance reports, with damage recorded on digital camera
- Weekly internal property inspection
- Appliance testing
- Airing of property
- Watering/feeding of house plants
- Small DIY tasks like changing light bulbs and fixing leaking taps
- Obtaining quotes for repair work
- Meeting and briefing trades people, checking their work and locking up after them
- Arranging/overseeing building works
- Gardening
- Pool cleaning
- Painting and decorating

absent owners, and if they look less than perfectly maintained – or are only able or willing to show you an almost brand new property – you will know to look elsewhere.

Make sure you agree a properly written contract with any management company that you employ, and ensure the contract has an opt-out clause that entitles you to end the relationship with the company quickly if the arrangement does not work as planned.

Depending on precisely what services you require – and it pays to be clear about your exact expectations from the start – expect to pay in the region of 0.5 to 0.8% of the purchase price per year for property management. A monthly clean of a generally unoccupied property (that is, not taking into account changing and washing bedding and towels, for example) would probably add another 0.1 to 0.2% of purchase price to your costs.

Buyers in remote areas where there may not be an abundance of property management companies may do well to ingratiate themselves subtly with neighbours, who can be surprisingly helpful.

SWIMMING POOLS

Swimming pools come in all shapes and sizes, and most are expensive – both to install and to maintain. The cheapest option is an above-ground prefabricated pool, with below-ground liner pools more expensive and reinforced concrete tiled pools the highest cost option. Depending on how grand a pool you require, the cost of installation could be anywhere upwards of £10,000, and may be extremely expensive if you involve an architect in the project and opt for a fully tiled pool.

Keeping a swimming pool in good condition requires continuous cleaning and filtering. Modern pools use filters to remove the dirt from the water, and sanitisers to kill any bacteria. Normally the water is removed from the pool through floor sumps and skimmers located at water level and then passed through the filters by means of the circulating pumps; and is sanitised, and if necessary heated, before returning to the pool via return water inlets located in the walls or floor.

There are many ways to sanitise pool water, the commonest being to chlorinate the water; but there are non-chemical techniques as well, involving ionisation and oxidisation.

Yearly pool maintenance contracts are popular among owners who do not live on site, and especially those whose

 If you share a pool as part of a complex, it will drive up the service charge, so think about this when viewing properties. See pages 66-74.

pool is used by paying guests – who may not take kindly to spending hours checking pH levels and cleaning the pool every few days.

Generally you will need to arrange for twice weekly pool cleaning during May to September, and a weekly visit during October to April. The maintenance person will monitor chemical levels closely and clear the pool of all floating debris. This should take less than an hour per visit. A yearly pool cleaning contract is likely to cost you around £500.

Safety issues

If you plan to let out a property with a swimming pool, it is sensible and in some places essential to ensure that it conforms to the relevant safety standards. This may create additional costs, particularly if you are installing a pool from scratch, but in an increasingly litigious world it could save you money in the long run.

In France in particular the authorities come down hard on failure to comply with swimming pool safety regulations and can in extreme cases impose heavy fines for non-compliance – so it is well worth asking your surveyor and/or pool installers for advice on the latest regulations.

Security products to consider include safety barriers, safety covers and pool alarms, all of which can provide valuable protection against children drowning.

Ask installers for written confirmation that their products comply with the latest standards, and keep copies of receipts for work carried out, and of your own and pool maintenance companies' checks.

GARDENS

Depending on the location and type of property you have bought, and your level of interest in horticulture, you may or may not have taken on responsibility for an overseas garden as well as a building.

Estate agents tend to be of the view that gardens do not, in and of themselves, add a huge amount to property values – but a neglected garden can certainly detract from an otherwise well-maintained property, and if you are going to be letting your

Common pool problems

It can be great to have a pool but keep an eye on the pH to avoid common problems.

Low pH balance causes:

Pitting of concrete
Metal to dissolve
Staining of walls
Skin/eye irritation

High pH causes:

Reduced water circulation
Cloudy pool water
Increased algae growth
Chlorine inefficiency
Skin/eye irritation

property out to tourists they will expect any outside space to be well looked after and attractive.

If you are building a house from scratch, are renovating an existing garden or have bought an off-plan property and will be creating a garden on your plot, try to invest no more than around 5% of the total property value in the garden. If you spend your money wisely, the garden may add disproportionately to its value and, if you are letting it out, help attract tenants.

Unless you are planning to live in the property full time, chances are you will want to create a garden that requires as little maintenance as possible, and as such you may want to bear in mind some golden rules of low-maintenance gardening (see box). If you plant carefully and use plenty of paving and gravelled spaces you could produce an attractive outside space which only requires a few hours' tender loving care every couple of months.

Especially if the property is in an area with a hot, dry climate, it may be particularly worthwhile to opt for drought-resistant plants like cacti, and to avoid planting in pots, which tend to require much more watering. Ground-cover plants, and gardens which make use of gravel, rockeries and raised beds can also help keep maintenance to a minimum.

If you are letting a property out to permanent tenants it may be possible to include a clause in the contract that provides for the tenant to maintain the garden, although this would generally not include pruning trees or large hedges. Do not expect tenants to take as much care with the garden as you might yourself, though, and expect to have to provide them with appropriate tools and equipment to encourage them to develop green fingers.

Many second home owners pay a gardener to maintain their gardens, and the cost of this will depend on the size of the plot. Depending on where you buy, you might expect a typical hourly rate to be around £10; assuming the garden is not overly elaborate you should be able to keep it looking good for around £200 a year.

Golden rules of low-maintenance gardening

- Choose plants that are known to be reliable and problem-free for your area and that will not outgrow the space you are working with.
- Reduce the size of your lawn or eliminate it entirely, using paving and/or gravelled areas instead.
- Prepare the soil well before planting so plants get a strong start.
- Mulch to reduce weeds and conserve soil moisture.
- If you live where watering is a necessity, install an automatic system, possibly drip.

Insuring your property

Tempting as it may be to take out standard home insurance policies when you buy overseas, most overseas property owners are better served by specialist policies that cover them during periods where the property is left unoccupied; is let out to permanent tenants; or is let out to tourists.

If you were to use a standard policy and fail to disclose that this is your second home, the insurer would be within its rights to refuse to pay out in the event of a claim. Look for policies which include the following:

BUILDINGS INSURANCE

If you are taking out a mortgage on your property the lender will insist that you have this cover. Buildings insurance covers the actual structure of your home for the cost of repairs or rebuilding, debris removal and professional fees following loss or damage caused by fire, storm, flood, burst pipes and subsidence. Fixtures and fittings within the buildings, such as kitchens and baths will also be covered. You need to insure for the cost of rebuilding the property, including outbuildings, garages, domestic oil and gas pipes, fuel tanks, swimming pools, drives, patios, terraces, walls, gates and fences. If you had a survey report done on the property, there should be a rebuild figure listed for insurance purposes; alternatively you could ask a local builder or surveyor to provide an insurance valuation. It is important to get this figure right as most insurers will index link, which means the sum insured will be adjusted yearly in line with the house rebuilding cost index.

CONTENTS INSURANCE

You may not have many expensive items in the property if you are only using it occasionally, but if you are letting it out to tourists you may need a considerable suite of 'mod cons' including satellite TV, CD and DVD players as well as suitable furniture and furnishings. You will need to calculate how much it would cost to replace your contents on a 'new for old' basis at today's prices. Especially if you are letting the property out, you will almost certainly want to include accidental damage cover in case you have careless tenants who cause damage.

LEGAL LIABILITY INSURANCE

Having public liability insurance offers vital protection if you are planning to let your home out. This covers you for legal costs and expenses following death, injury or damage to a third party on or near your property, and most agencies now insist that you have this cover. Look for policies with a minimum indemnity of £2 million.

EMPLOYERS' LIABILITY

It is a legal requirement that if you employ people while running a holiday-let business, you have employers liability insurance. This covers claims for death or injury to anyone you employ, for example a gardener, cleaner or handyman. Choose a policy with an indemnity limit of at least £3 million.

LOSS OF RENT

Unforeseen incidents may prevent you from letting your holiday home, so including 'loss of rent' cover means you could claim if, for example, the property was flooded and therefore inhabitable – and you not only lost rental income but also had to pay out for alternative accommodation for clients as a result. Another option is cancellation insurance, whereby you can claim if guests let you down.

LEGAL EXPENSES INSURANCE

This covers the cost of legal advice and proceedings, and can be useful if for example you end up in a legal dispute with one of your tenants, or with a letting agency. Policies provide cover up to a certain level of legal fees, for example £50,000.

Whatever policy you choose, always read the small print. There may be a clause that excludes cover if the house is uninhabited for more than a set number of consecutive days, for example, or when let to people outside your family; there may also be rules such as someone having to visit the property every week or particular kinds of locks and alarm systems being installed. Some insurers even insist on things like the heating system being drained when the property is left unoccupied, and the property being heated constantly to a certain minimum temperature.

If your holiday bookings are seasonal, you may wish to let your second home on a six-month lease during winter months, rather than leave it standing empty. Make sure that your insurance allows you to do so.

Policies for properties under long term tenancies should offer a similar level of cover, although you may not need to include accidental damage cover as you will have taken a month's worth of rent in advance by way of damage deposit.

UK insurers

It is probably cheaper to insure your property with a local company, but you may prefer to use a UK firm. Make sure you take out a policy that includes emergency travel expenses if you need to fly out following a disaster.

Letting your property out

Whether to tourists or long-term tenants, if you let your property out there will be a host of issues you need to grapple with. A few of the most important ones are outlined below. Look back to Chapter 1 for advice on rental income and calculating rental yield.

If you have friends who let out properties they should be able to furnish you with a huge variety of salutary lessons and anecdotes to send you on your way into the wonderful world of property lettings. These may or may not be useful, but it is certainly helpful to approach your

❝ Do not expect your property to be full all year round and at peak rates. ❞

business with an open mind, and to soak up as much help from books, websites and small business advisers as possible as you go along.

SETTING REALISTIC TARGETS

Many people buy a holiday home thinking they will have no problem letting it out throughout the year, at just about any price they choose. This has never been the case, and if anything the market is becoming ever-more competitive, thanks to the growth in numbers of people buying second homes and letting them out.

The longest letting seasons are in places that have a sunny climate all year round, like the Canary Islands; or in perennially popular cultural hotspots, like Paris or Venice – but even in these areas, do not expect your property to be full all year round and at peak rates.

In areas where your main market is likely to be families heading for the sun during the school holidays, you might be doing well if you fill the property for more than 12 weeks – although if that is the case, you will probably need to hold out for maximum rent levels and minimise the number of void days if at all possible.

The key to running a successful overseas lettings business is to be realistic, to know what you want the business to achieve, and to know your market. How many weeks per year do you want/need the property to be let, how much are people prepared to spend on staying in a property like yours, and what do they expect for that money?

If you want to do really well and be sure of always filling your allotted rental weeks, you may need to steal a march on your competition, either by making your property that little bit more luxurious or stylish, or by focusing on offering a higher quality or more easily accessible service than your competitors do.

Remember that no matter how many people would like to rent your property for a particular week in August, only one group will ever be able to – so your aim is not to end up with vast numbers of people interested in summer lets, but rather to attract a reasonable number of clients throughout the year, with the summer as the likely peak season but

> ❝ Aim to attract a reasonable number of clients throughout the year. ❞

other mini-peaks occurring in each school holiday and – if you are doing well – throughout the period from March to October.

Bear in mind that continuing to run the lettings business year-round might prove uneconomical because of the expenses involved, in which case you might prefer to cut your losses and look for long-term tenants to take the property over the winter period

Landlord and tenant law in Europe

In much of Europe, tenants are better protected in law than is the case in England and Wales – particularly if they are renting on a long lease.

In these circumstances the earliest the landlord can ask the tenant to leave the property may be after as many as three years, whereas the tenant need only give a few months' notice. There are plenty of horror stories of people buying properties with sitting tenants and discovering that they have little or no legal power to evict them; your lawyer should have advised you on your legal rights before buying if such a tenant existed, and will be able to help if you are planning to rent the property out yourself.

Particularly with shorter, furnished lets it may be possible to make more informal arrangements, but ask your lawyer for advice if you are unsure of what you can and cannot do.

Bear in mind that depending on what and where you are buying, rent levels may be quite tightly controlled. In France, for example, the law says that even at the end of a lease landlords can only increase the rent level in line with changes to the building cost index; if they have made demonstrable improvements to the property since the departure of the previous tenant; or if the rent was obviously under-valued.

instead. This is a common tactic in parts of Spain and southern France.

GO IT ALONE OR APPOINT A LETTINGS AGENT?

A choice all property letters face is whether to manage the lettings business themselves, or to delegate the work to agency specialising in lettings management.

Looking after your own bookings may appear on the surface to be a straightforward job, but it is a multi-faceted one which can take up a surprising amount of time – especially when you first take over ownership of

> **"By going it alone you could, in theory, save money. "**

the property and are getting used to your new responsibilities.

The biggest problem with paying a lettings agent may be the effect of their fees on your bottom line.

If you are planning to let out your property on a long term tenancy, the letting agency is likely to want commission of at least 10% of what the tenant pays you in rent, and if tourist rentals is your game, you can expect to pay twice that. With cleaning costs added in, that means a quarter of your turnover will be taken

up before you even get to pay property management fees and taxes.

By going it alone you could, in theory, save money then. But where would you get your tenants from, and who would keep on top of the administrative side – taking bookings, banking cheques and handling complaints, for example? Who would hand over the keys to tenants and make sure that the cleaners were coming in on the right days and doing their job effectively?

If you do not already have a job you may be happy to deal with all this from a distance, and indeed maximising income from the property may be part of your wider career plans, so you may have no choice but to muddle through without paying an agent.

Alternatively you may feel you simply do not have the time to do the job justice, and it could be that you feel it is only by paying an agent that you stand any chance of achieving a reasonable level of lettings in the first place.

Either way, you will need to keep a close eye on the lettings business to make sure it is meeting whatever goal you have for it – whether that be for the property to 'wash its face' by generating enough letting income to cover mortgage payments and other

 Letting agency fees can be as high as 20% for holiday lets. For more on the impact of on-going costs, see page 27.

Services you may want from a letting agency

✓ Advertising the property

✓ Dealing with enquiries from clients

✓ Vetting clients to make sure they are suitable

✓ Handling client queries and complaints

✓ Keeping booking calendars and availability charts

✓ Keeping spreadsheet records of all rentals

✓ Managing bookings, taking and banking deposits and payments

✓ Holding damage deposits and making any necessary deductions

✓ Issuing clients with booking details, directions and arrival instructions

✓ Meeting and greeting, and briefing on local attractions and amenities, if required

✓ Arranging airport transfers if required

✓ Providing welcome packs if required

✓ Post-letting cleaning, laundry, rubbish disposal, inventory check

✓ Spring-clean at the beginning and end of the season

costs, or for it to bring in enough money for you to downshift to a four-day week and retain the same income level.

Many owners stress that even if you do use a lettings agent, it is well worth doing your own marketing yourself; this may feel counter-productive because you are helping the agent do the job you are already paying them to do, but the more

> " Normally, if your letting business makes a loss, you can carry it forward to a later year. "

business you can build up yourself, through family, friends, colleagues and perhaps a well-promoted website, the more likely you are to be able to stand on your own two feet and run the lettings yourself in the future.

Before you sign a contract with any agency, find out how you stand in terms of personal usage of the property – would there be any

restrictions on when you could use it? What happens if you generate bookings through friends or colleagues? If you set up your own website will you be able to publicise this through the agent?

DEALING WITH TAX

If you let your property out you will be liable to tax on all the profits – including the income it generates and any gain in capital when you come to sell it – both in the country in which it is located and in the UK. If there is a double taxation treaty between the two countries, what you have paid abroad will be deducted from any liability you have here, however.

To find out how to file tax returns in the country where the property is located, you will need to contact the local tax office. Tax rates, and the way foreign owners letting out their properties are dealt with, vary. For more information on individual countries, see Chapter 8.

Income tax

In terms of the UK taxman, you can deduct certain expenses and tax allowances from your rental income to work out your taxable profit (or loss).

The expenses you can deduct from letting income include:

- Letting agent fees.
- Legal fees for lets of a year or less, or for renewing a lease for less than 50 years.
- Accountant fees.

Check up on your letting agent

- Find out exactly where the agent advertises and ask for details of response rates
- Ask for phone numbers of other owners who use the agent and quiz them privately about how effective the agent is
- Ask a friend to do some 'mystery shopper' enquiries to the agent and report back on how quickly and effectively the agent responded

- Buildings and contents insurance.
- Interest on property loans.
- Maintenance and repairs (but not improvements).
- Utility bills (like gas, water, electricity).
- Rent, ground rent and service charges.
- Local taxes.
- Services you pay for, like cleaning or gardening.
- Other direct costs of letting the property, like phone calls, stationery and advertising costs.

Bear in mind that you can only claim expenses that are solely for running your property letting business. If the expense is only partly for running your business or if you use the property yourself then you may only be able to claim part of it.

Expenses that are non-allowable for UK tax purposes include:

- 'Capital' costs, like furniture or the property itself.
- Personal expenses – costs that are not to do with your letting business.
- Any loss you make when you sell the property.

There are certain allowances you can claim though, which can reduce your liability. These include:

- Capital allowances – a proportion of spending on assets like furniture may be offset against tax each year, and for things you need to run the property letting business, like cleaning and gardening equipment (usually you claim 50% in the first year and 25% for the next two years).
- Wear and tear allowance or a 'renewals' allowance.

You have to allocate expenses to the year they apply to – it does not matter when you actually pay them. Sometimes you may have to allocate part of an expense to one year and part to another.

Normally, if your letting business makes a loss, you can carry it forward to a later year and offset it against your future profits from the same business.

Capital gains tax

If, when you sell or give away an asset it has increased in value, you could be taxable on the 'gain' (profit). This does not apply when you sell personal belongings worth £6,000 or less or, in most cases, your main home.

Exemptions from CGT include:

- Your car.
- Your main home, provided certain conditions are met.

Formed in April 2005 from the merger of the Inland Revenue and HM Customs and Excise, HM Revenue & Customs is the authority to contact for advice on your UK tax affairs. Website: www.hmrc.gov.uk

- ISAs or PEPs.
- UK Government gilts (bonds).
- Personal belongings worth £6,000 or less when you sell them.
- Betting, lottery or pools winnings.
- Money which forms part of your income for income tax purposes, so a second home is liable.

It is worth bearing in mind that:

- If you are married or in a civil partnership and living together you can transfer assets to your husband, wife or civil partner without having to pay CGT.
- You cannot give assets to your children or others or sell them assets cheaply without having to consider CGT.
- If you make a loss you may be able to make a claim to deduct that loss from other gains; but only if the asset normally attracts CGT – thus you cannot set a loss on selling your car against gains from disposing of other assets.
- If someone dies and leaves their belongings to their beneficiaries, there is no CGT to pay at that time – however if an asset is later disposed of by a beneficiary, any CGT they may have to pay will be based on the difference between the market value at the time of death and the value at the time of disposal.

CGT is worked out for each tax year, and is charged on the total of your taxable gains, after taking into account:

- Certain costs and reliefs that can reduce or defer gains.
- Allowable losses you have made on assets to which normally CGT applies.
- The annual exempt (tax-free) amount (set by the Chancellor in the annual budget).

How much CGT you pay depends on your overall income and the size of the gain. Your total taxable gains are added to your taxable income for the year and treated as the top part of that total and taxed accordingly. So if the gain pushes you into the higher rate tax bracket, you must pay the relevant going rate.

Minimising your tax bill

There are plenty of legitimate ways of minimising the amount you owe the taxman as a result of adding an overseas property to your assets, without 'dodging' tax. You will hopefully have spoken to your financial adviser and lawyer about the tax implications before buying the property; if not, or if your circumstances change, contact a specialist tax accountant for further advice.

WHAT RECORDS YOU NEED TO KEEP

You need to keep the same sorts of records whatever type of property letting business you have – residential or holiday letting, in the UK or overseas. They should include details of your rental income, allowable expenses and 'capital' costs.

- Rental income – keep a note of the rent you charge and receive and the dates you rent out the property.

- Allowable expenses – your records should include details of all your costs of letting or managing your property (as outlined above).

- 'Capital' costs – keep a record of relevant assets, how much they cost and when you bought them.

To back up your records keep rent books, receipts, invoices and bank statements. Also make sure that you can separate your business from your personal expenses.

Note that if your total income is under £15,000 a year before expenses, you can group the expenses as a single total on your tax return. If it is £15,000 or more, you will need to show them separately and complete the full return. Your Tax Office can ask to see your records at any time.

If you make a profit when you sell a property that is not your main home you may have to pay CGT, but some of your property costs can be deducted when working out your gain, so you will need a record of:

- when you bought and sold it

- the purchase and sale price

- buying and selling costs, like Stamp Duty and legal fees

- improvement costs and dates

Bear in mind that record keeping requirements may be different in the country where your property is located, and that the tax year in most countries apart from the UK runs from 1 January to 31 December. You may also need to keep other records to show that your property is safe to let out.

PAYING LOCAL TAXES

Wherever you buy, you will be liable for local property taxes that are similar in nature to UK council tax, and like in the UK, are intended to cover various types of local public services including street lighting and sewerage; they also vary significantly according to where you buy.

Such capitation-style taxes must be paid by the person who lives in the property – so if you are letting it out on a long term tenancy, your tenant will pay, but otherwise you will be liable. There may be reductions if you are renovating the property and it is therefore uninhabitable, or if you are retired.

In some countries you will have to pay a land tax, which is charged regardless of whether there is anyone living at the property. Each property owner's contribution is calculated on the declared value of the property.

You may also need to pay a separate rubbish tax and water rates, again payable to the local council.

The total cost of all these taxes will be similar to or, more often than not, less than what you might expect to pay in the UK – perhaps 0.5% of the declared value of the property per year.

Bear in mind though that depending on the kind of property you bought, you may also be paying community fees that fund, amongst other things, street lighting and cleaning in the local area. This is particular to your development and is additional to what the council provides.

Using a gestor

Bureaucracy in Spain and Portugal is considered legendary in its complexity, and many people employ the services of a *gestor* - a kind of intermediary between the individual and the state. He or she will be knowledgeable about what procedures you need to comply with, and may even supply you with the relevant forms - for example for social security-related issues or even for apparently simple things like registering your car. If you have bought in either of these countries and are not sure what local taxes you are liable for and how to pay, ask a licensed *gestor* and they will set you right.

Moving abroad

Moving abroad involves making an overseas property your main residence. For some people this entails working overseas and enrolling their children in local schools, for others it is the culmination of long-cherished retirement plans, for which the purchase of a holiday home was a taste of things to come.

Pastures new

For many owners, buying abroad is about a holiday home, for others it is the start of a complete relocation overseas. If this is the case, there are many additional factors to consider, from work and taxation to healthcare, pensions and inheritance.

Emigration might have been your reason for buying abroad in the first place; alternatively after a few years of owning a second home overseas you may find you have developed a taste for foreign culture and want to move away from the UK on a more permanent basis.

Either way, moving abroad is likely to be a big upheaval for you and your family, so it is important to think carefully about all aspects of the move before you make any firm decisions.

❝ One barrier to earning a living abroad could be whether or not you can get your qualifications recognised. ❞

WORK AND TAX

If you are below retirement age one of the most important issues you are likely to have to deal with is how to earn money in the country you are thinking about moving to; and as a knock-on effect you will need to handle your tax affairs appropriately.

Qualifications

Depending on the kind of work you do, one potential barrier to earning a living could be whether or not you can get your qualifications recognised. Within the European Economic Area your diploma and other professional qualifications should, in theory, be recognised as they stand. Recognition is not granted automatically though.

In practice, if you are recognised as fully qualified to practise in a regulated profession in one country, you should be allowed to practise the same profession in another country. Regulated professions are those that are legally restricted by the state or professional bodies to people with certain qualifications – for example, medicine, the law, teaching and accountancy. 'Fully qualified' in this context means having gained a professional qualification after at least three years of higher-level, post-secondary education.

Directives provide that for seven professions – medicine, nursing, dentistry, midwifery, veterinary surgery, pharmacy and architecture – there can be no restrictions on practising in another EEA country, other than the imposition of a language test.

For unregulated professions, and if you are hoping to work in a country outside the EEA, recognition of qualifications will be a matter for the competent authority in the country in question, and there is much scope for dispute, especially if there is a disparity between how people working in your field are trained in your soon-to-be-adopted country and how you have been trained in the UK.

As a starting point, find out how your qualifications are viewed by other countries by contacting the relevant National Academic Recognition Information Centre. To compare vocational qualifications within Europe, contact the European Centre for the Development of Vocational Training. If you do want to get proof of equivalence of qualifications, you will need to get certified, translated copies of your diplomas and certificates with original stamps and signatures, and any other documents to support your case. You will generally need to apply to the ministry of education to have your qualifications recognised.

Finding work

None of this guarantees that there will be a job waiting for you – and there are as many ways of looking for work

overseas as there are in the UK, ranging from networking to reading classified ads and visiting the local equivalent of job centres.

One useful source of help is a collaboration between the employment services of EU member states and of countries in the EEA, which together operate the European Employment Services Network (EURES). This has around 500 staff trained to deal with cross-border job seekers. Vacancies and details of local contacts for each country can be found on the EURES website.

Remember that when you move abroad you will no longer have the career-related safety net which you probably take for granted in the UK but which is forged out of:

- Fixed and known career paths.
- Knowledge of what qualifications and experience are needed for what jobs.

European Employment Services (EURES) is the network linking public employment services in Europe. Its role is to help people move freely and take up work in other member states of the European Economic Area (EEA). Website: www.eu.int/eures

135

- Knowledge of alternative sources of income and training opportunities.
- Ease of access to advice.
- Ease of handling job applications.
- A network of personal contacts.

You may be the kind of person who enjoys the challenge of 'making it' on your own in a new country; if you are not, try to lay as much groundwork as possible before you move.

At first you may find a relatively simple source of income is to try to make money through using your English language skills – either in some sort of teaching role, or in working for or setting up a business aimed at other expatriates.

Completing a 'teaching English as a foreign language' (TEFL) course before going abroad is a good way of finding out if you would like to teach abroad, and gives you an internationally recognised qualification. For information on relevant courses and qualifications, visit www.europa-pages.com/uk/index.html and follow the links to TEFL qualifications and UK TEFL courses.

If you are considering working for yourself or running any kind of business, make sure you research in advance whether or not there is a market for your skills or idea. Ensure you deal with all the relevant paperwork too; it is likely that as any kind of small business person you will need to be registered with the local chamber of commerce, for example, which will involve an upfront fee.

PAYING TAX

Even though you may feel like an émigré the moment you step off the plane, the UK taxman may be rather more reluctant to accept that you have left for good.

Before you leave you should inform your tax office and ask for a form P85, which will let the Inland Revenue know of your plans. But it is important to understand that this may not fundamentally change your tax status overnight.

If you leave the UK to work full-time abroad under a contract of employment, you are treated as not resident and not 'ordinarily resident' (see box below) from the day after you leave the UK until the day before you return to the UK at the end of your employment abroad, if you meet all the following conditions:

- Your absence from the UK and your employment abroad both last for at least a whole tax year.
- During your absence any visits you make to the UK
  – total less than 183 days in any tax year, and

Formed in April 2005 from the merger of the Inland Revenue and HM Customs and Excise, HM Revenue & Customs is the authority to contact for advice on your UK tax affairs. Website: www.hmrc.gov.uk

– average less than 91 days a tax year (worked out over the period of absence up to a maximum of four years).

Otherwise, you will normally continue to be considered a UK resident for tax purposes until:

- You have been absent from the UK for a complete tax year (6 April to 5 April), during which you spent less than 183 days in the UK during the tax year, and
- Your visits to the UK do not average 91 days or more per tax year over a maximum of four years.

If under this definition you continue to be UK resident (or ordinarily resident) after your departure, you will be taxable here on your income arising in the UK and overseas, which means – depending on how your new country treats you tax-wise, that you may end up paying tax to both jurisdictions. But depending on the terms of any

❝Even though you may feel like an émigré, the UK taxman may be reluctant to accept that you have left for good.❞

double taxation treaty with the UK, you should be able to reclaim the tax you have paid in one country when the other one works out how much you owe it.

If you tell the Inland Revenue that you are neither resident nor ordinarily resident in the UK, they may ask you to prove that you have left permanently, or intend to live outside the UK for three years or more. This evidence might be, for example, that you have bought an overseas property to live in as a permanent home. If you continue to have property in the UK for your use, you will need to show that your reason for doing so is consistent with your stated aim of living abroad permanently or for three years or more.

Tax on rental income in the UK

If you hold onto your UK property and let it out, you will be taxable on any profit you make. Where you receive rental income direct from the tenant, they should first deduct tax at the basic rate and pay it to the Inland Revenue. Where a letting agent collects the rental income for you, the letting agent must deduct tax at the basic rate from the income received less the allowable expenses paid on your behalf. In either case you can set off the tax against your UK income tax liability when you complete your tax return. You may apply for the rent to be paid to you without deduction of tax. For more information, ask your tax office for leaflet IR140. If gross payment of rent is approved, you will still be liable to tax on your net profit.

If you have left the UK permanently or for at least three years, you will be treated as not resident and not ordinarily resident from the day after the date of your departure.

Bear in mind that even as a non-resident, you will still be taxable in the UK on any income arising in the UK, which may include:

- Interest from a UK bank or building society account.
- Interest paid by a UK company.
- Dividends from a UK company.
- Interest on UK Government securities (gilts).
- Income from property in the UK.
- UK pensions or annuities.

For more information on your tax liabilities following a move abroad, contact the Inland Revenue's Centre for Non-Residents.

ORDINARY RESIDENCE

Your liability for UK tax may be affected by the concept of 'ordinary residence', which the Inland Revenue uses to take account of the fact that you might leave the UK and live abroad for a while but still be attached to the UK to an extent that you should pay taxes here.

In order to avoid being liable for capital gains tax here, for example, you would normally need to be not resident and not ordinarily resident in the UK for at least five full tax years

Ordinary residence for social security purposes

The definition of 'ordinary residence' is different for social security purposes. Here are a few pointers:

Factor	Indication of
You return to the UK from time to time while you are employed abroad	Continued ordinary residence – the more frequent the returns, the stronger the indication
Visits to your family who live in your UK home; or holidays in your UK home	Ordinary residence
Partner and/or children are with you during your overseas employment	Not being ordinarily resident, particularly if you do not retain a home in the UK or only make occasional visits
You maintain a home in the UK	Ordinary residence
Your UK home is rented on a long let	Not being ordinarily resident
You will return to the UK at the end of your employment overseas	Ordinary residence – the earlier you will return, the stronger the indication

between the year you left the UK and the year of your return.

Deciding whether or not you are 'ordinarily resident' will be up to the Inland Revenue's Centre for Non-Residents to decide, and it is important to understand that it is possible to be resident (or ordinarily resident) in both the UK and another country (or countries) at the same time. If you are resident (or ordinarily resident) in another country, this does not mean that you cannot also be resident (or ordinarily resident) in the UK for tax purposes.

Just to complicate things, 'ordinary residence' is defined differently for social security purposes (see box, left). For more information, contact the relevant authorities.

SOCIAL SECURITY

European Community regulations mean that if you move within the European Economic Area your benefit rights are protected, so long as you:

- are employed or self-employed
- have been employed or self-employed and are getting benefit, or
- are a student studying or receiving vocational training leading to an officially recognised qualification – although in this case, only limited rights arise.

This means you can claim the contribution-based part of the Jobseeker's Allowance for up to three months after leaving the UK, although

you must follow your new country's rules about looking for work. Once you have been working in the new country and paying into their social insurance scheme you may be entitled to their unemployment benefits.

Maternity allowance and short-term incapacity benefit are also payable, as is long-term sickness benefit. Attendance and carers' allowances and Disability Living Allowance will not be paid, however, and you will only get UK Child Allowance if you remain employed by a UK employer (although you should get the local equivalent if you are working and paying social insurance).

If you work in another EEA country for an EEA employer (this includes a UK employer), or as someone who is self-employed, you will usually need to be insured under the social security laws of the country you work in and will not usually have to pay UK NI contributions.

This is not always the case, though. For example if you work for a UK employer in another EEA country for less than 12 months, you will generally continue to pay UK National Insurance contributions.

There are some countries outside the EEA with which the UK has two-way social security agreements (see box). If you are moving to one of these countries, your employer has a place of business in the UK and you are 'ordinarily resident' in the UK (the definition of which may be different from that for tax purposes, see box), you must continue to pay Class 1 NI contributions for the first 52 weeks you are there. If not, there will be a gap in your insurance record, which could affect your entitlement to benefits.

After this period – and even if you are insured under your new country's social security scheme – you may still want to make 'voluntary contributions' to the UK NI scheme, because they may help you get a UK state pension and some other UK benefits.

It is important to take advice on all this as soon as you know you are likely to be moving abroad permanently – if in doubt, speak to a suitably qualified accountant. If you do want to pay voluntary contributions to the UK NI scheme, you will need to inform the Inland Revenue as soon as possible, because you must pay your voluntary contributions within certain time limits for them to count for benefit. Bear in mind that you may not be able to pay voluntary contributions to the UK scheme if you are already paying voluntary contributions in another country.

Countries with social security agreements in place

Various countries have various arrangements set up with the UK. These countries are:

Countries covered by EC social security agreements

Austria	Gibraltar (for	Latvia	Slovakia
Belgium	everything except	Liechtenstein	Slovenia
Cyprus	healthcare and	Lithuania	Spain
Czech Republic	child benefits)	Luxembourg	Sweden
Denmark	Greece	Malta	Switzerland (not a
Estonia	Hungary	Netherlands	member of the EEA, but
Finland	Iceland	Norway	EU rules on social
France	Ireland	Poland	security also apply)
Germany	Italy	Portugal	United Kingdom

Other countries with reciprocal social security agreements

Barbados	Jamaica	New Zealand
Bermuda	Japan*	Philippines
Bosnia-Herzegovina	Jersey/Guernsey	Serbia/Montenegro
Canada*	Korea*	Turkey
Croatia	Macedonia	USA
Israel	Mauritius	

* Agreement has limited scope

Looking after your family

Issues that you probably take for granted in the UK, like access to benefits, schools and healthcare, require forward planning and organisation when you are planning to move abroad. It is well worth giving them plenty of thought before you go too far down the road towards a decision to emigrate.

FINDING SCHOOLS

If you have children of school age you will need to find them a suitable school in your adopted home.

Local schools

Depending on a variety of factors, including their age and your perception of how good the local education system is, you may decide to throw them in at the deep end and attend a local school, where lessons will be conducted in the local language.

If so you may want to arrange for some basic language lessons for them in advance, so they do not feel completely bewildered by what is going on in class or in the playground. Do not necessarily expect a huge amount of extra support for them within mainstream classes.

Bear in mind that there is likely to be little transferability in terms of the style and content of education received abroad and in the UK, so if you are in any doubt about whether or not your family is going to stay in your new location, think carefully about whether this is the most sensible option.

> **❝ Arrange basic language lessons for yourself and your children as soon as you arrive in your new country. ❞**

International schools

Another option might be some sort of international school – these are generally English-speaking schools in non-English speaking countries, where a proportion of the children (perhaps as low as a fifth) come from expatriate families, with the rest being wealthy locals. Fees can be high.

 To find out more about the state education system in your new country, talk to the local council or visit the relevant government website. See Chapter 8.

Some international schools, which tend to be located in cities or areas where there is a high concentration of expatriates, follow a UK curriculum and may even be known as the British School; others follow US or internationally agreed standards. For further information, contact the Council of International Schools (website www.cois.org) which accredits international schools across the world or the Council of British International Schools, which covers the EU (www.cobisec.org).

ACCESSING HEALTHCARE

Apart from for the first 12 months of taking up employment with a UK employer, or of self-employment, in another EEA country, you will usually have to pay into a state sickness insurance fund or a private healthcare scheme, depending on the law of that country, when you move abroad. You will need to present the local authorities with your completed E106 form to register for the scheme.

If you remain insured in the UK rather than in the new country – for example during the first twelve months of working for a UK employer overseas, or if you are living but not working there – you will be able to get healthcare under the other country's scheme as though you were insured there, for that temporary period. You will need a European Health Insurance Card (previously the E111, or for pensioners, E121), obtainable from main post offices, as proof of eligibility to equivalent cover.

In some EEA countries, you may not have to pay into a state sickness insurance scheme if you work for an employer but earn more or less than a certain amount, or if you are self-employed. Check with the relevant authorities to see if this applies to you. If it does, you may be able to pay voluntary contributions to their scheme. If you cannot, you should think about taking out private medical insurance.

❝Some international schools follow a UK curriculum and may even be known as the British School.❞

The Council of International Schools is a worldwide association of schools and post-secondary institutions; the European council of International Schools, Council of International Schools in the Americas and the Council of Internationally Accredited Schools (Australia) are also accessible via www.cois.org

It is your responsibility to see that you have healthcare cover, so if you are no longer paying UK NI contributions and are not insured in your new country, you will have to pay all your healthcare costs in full on a private basis. Whatever your situation, remember that in some EEA countries, you may have to pay part or all of the costs of some services which are free of charge

Non-EEA countries with healthcare agreements for UK visitors

Australia, Barbados, British Dependent Territories (such as British Virgin Islands, Montserrat and St Helena), Bulgaria, Channel Islands, Gibraltar, New Zealand, Romania, some former USSR republics (including Armenia, Moldova, Russia and Ukraine) and the former Yugoslavia (Serbia/Montenegro, Croatia, Bosnia and Macedonia).

Jargon buster

EHIC European Health Insurance Card (formerly E111), available from Post Offices and online via the DWP website. This provides necessary treatment, at the same cost as the locals would pay, for those on temporary visits to other EU/EEA states and Switzerland.

E106 If you move abroad within the EEA or Switzerland and are below retirement age, an E106 form will, depending on the amount of National Insurance contributions paid during your working career, entitle you to an extension of EHIC cover for a period of up to two years. You must register with the social security office and bring documentation such as passport, proofs of residence etc.

E121 Like the E106 form, this acts as an extension of the EHIC entitlement, for people in receipt of a UK state pension.

under the NHS. For more information, ask your local tax office for a copy of leaflet SA29.

If you are visiting certain countries outside the EEA you may be able to get some free or subsidised emergency treatment (see box, above), but this provision is not intended for permanent residents.

In other countries you will have to pay even for emergency care, so it is essential to have private travel insurance as a temporary visitor and you will need to make more permanent arrangements as a resident. Bear in mind that costs of private healthcare in some countries – including the US – can be prohibitively high.

Remember also that even within the EEA and the countries with reciprocal agreements, you will not be covered for the costs of repatriation unless you have separate, private healthcare insurance.

143

Retiring abroad

If you plan to retire overseas, you will need to be as clear as possible about what income you will have to live on. Many people relocate partly because they feel the cost of living in other countries is cheaper than in the UK, but this does not mean you can live on air!

PLANNING FOR RETIREMENT

Pension planning is a complex task at any time, and even more so if you factor in the potential disruption caused by moving abroad and therefore changing tax jurisdictions.

Pension forecasts

If you are further than four months away from UK state pension age, you can ask the Inland Revenue for a forecast of what UK state pension you can expect to get.

For occupational or personal pension schemes, you should already receive regular benefit statements which should give you an idea of how much income you will have in retirement – although bear in mind that any forecast is based on certain assumptions, like the average inflation rate between now and your retirement date.

Armed with the information provided in these forecasts, you should ideally consult a financial adviser specialising in retirement planning before you start planning to move abroad.

By the time you move abroad you should have a clear picture of what your likely pension income will be. If you are some way off retirement this will help you plan whether to continue to pay into UK pensions and at what point it may be advisable to start paying into an overseas pension; if you are near retirement age it will allow you to plan your post-emigration finances more effectively.

Continuing contributions

If you are still of working age, one issue to talk to your advisers about is whether to continue paying voluntary National Insurance contributions in order to receive the full UK state pension (see earlier section on social security contributions). Beyond this, you will need to think about what to do in terms of your existing occupational and/or private pension schemes.

Under the current rules, which came in as of 6 April 2006, anyone can become or remain a member of a UK approved pension scheme, regardless of nationality and UK tax treatment, as long as the scheme's rules allow.

But tax relief on member contributions will only be available to people who:

- are chargeable to UK tax
- are tax resident in the UK (see the section on paying tax, above), or
- were resident in the UK in one of the previous five tax years and, at the time they were resident, became members of a UK registered pension scheme.

If you meet these requirements and have 'UK relevant earnings' of more than a minimum limit (£3,600 in 2006/07), you can get tax relief on contributions up to the lower of 100% of salary and the level of the current annual pensions allowance. If your earnings are lower than the minimum you will only get tax relief on contributions up to that limit. Tax relief on employer contributions will be available in the normal way up to the level of the annual allowance for as long as the employer remains UK resident.

In other words, you can retain the status quo in terms of your pension contributions for up to five years after moving abroad. After that, you will no longer get tax relief on your pension payments, so it is unlikely that continuing with your UK pension will be your most tax-efficient option. You may want to start an overseas pension at that point; or you may prefer to make some other form of provision for your retirement.

❝ You can claim your UK state pension in any other EEA country, or a country with a reciprocal agreement with the UK. ❞

CLAIMING YOUR STATE PENSION

You can claim your UK state pension in any other EEA country, or a country with a reciprocal agreement with the UK (see box on page x). You will get the same pension as you would if you had stayed in the UK.

The Pension Service will usually send you a claim form about four months before you reach UK state pension age – assuming you have given them your new address. The form will ask you if you want to claim a UK state pension. It also asks you for information about any insurance and residence you may have in other countries.

If you have also paid sufficient contributions to your new country's scheme, you should also be eligible for a pension from it, although bear in mind that the rules on required levels of contribution and the age at which you can start to claim pensions vary between countries.

CLAIMING OTHER PENSIONS

If you have a personal or occupational pension, moving abroad should not have any effect on your ability to receive payments when you retire.

145

Your pension should be paid in full and you are normally entitled to any rises regardless of the country you retire to.

But check the details of your scheme carefully before you move. In particular check whether your scheme will pay into an overseas bank account – some company schemes will only pay into a UK bank; and find out whether your annuity company will transfer money overseas free of charge – some companies will charge you for each overseas payment.

Remember that one issue you will face when you come to receive your pension income is currency risk. Your pension will be paid in sterling, so as exchange rates fluctuate, your income will vary from month to month.

Some providers are willing to avoid this situation by paying in local currency, and the number of providers prepared to do this, particularly in euros, is expected to increase in the future.

If you are sure you are going to be staying abroad, it may be worth exercising your 'open market option'. This allows you to buy your annuity from the provider of your choice – partly on the basis of whether it will pay out in local currency – not just the one who holds your funds.

Another issue to think about is whether to shift other savings into the local currency, partly for the sake of convenience and partly so your entire nest-egg is not exposed to currency risk.

TAX ON YOUR PENSION

Remember that you are liable to UK tax on your UK pension income, and it may also be subject to tax in the country in which you live.

You will not be liable to UK tax on your UK pension if you live in a country which has a double taxation agreement with the UK which exempts UK pensions from UK tax. Where that is the case, and you make a claim for relief, the Inland Revenue will authorise payment of your pension without deduction of tax.

> ↘ The Pension Service International Pension Centre deals with queries about United Kingdom benefits payable to overseas customers. You can contact the IPC on +44 191 218 7777 or fax +44 191 218 7293. Opening hours are 8.00 am to 8.00 pm (GMT). Or you can write to The International Pension Centre, Tyneview Park, Newcastle Upon Tyne, NE98 1BA, United Kingdom.

Arranging the move

If you are keeping your UK home and renting it out, you may get away with transporting your possessions in a self-drive van to your new home. Otherwise, you will need to use a company that specialises in international removals.

As when choosing a builder, ask around for recommendations of which firms are reliable, and get at least three written quotations if possible. Ask for detailed prices, and for details about how they pack and deal with any valuable or fragile items. Removals will generally be charged by the cubic metre, and you will probably have to spend several thousand pounds to move a whole house-worth of possessions.

Make sure you have full insurance for the whole journey; many removal companies offer their own policies but you may prefer to add extra cover to your existing home contents policy. Whatever policy you choose, check the small print carefully, keeping a particular eye out for exclusions.

Look for companies which are members of the British Association of Removers (www.bar.co.uk) and one of two international bodies, the

Who to notify of your move

- If you are keeping your property in the UK and it is going to be empty or rented out, you will need to let your mortgage lender and insurance providers know
- Contact your local council – their council tax department and electoral registration unit will need to know when you are leaving and a forwarding address
- Notify your utility companies that you are moving in order to get your final bills and provide a forwarding address for them to send you any outstanding payments or refunds
- Tell your bank, building society or any financial institution that you have a policy or agreement with that you are moving abroad
- Have your mail forwarded by asking for a re-direction form at a Post Office – allow enough time for this to be set up as it can take a few weeks
- If you have children, notify the school and the local education authority of the date when you will be withdrawing them from school

Fédération Internationale des Déménageurs Internationaux (www.fidi.com) or the Overseas Moving Network International (www.omnimoving.com), both of which offer bonded guarantee schemes.

Taking your pet

Before leaving the UK, your dog or cat must be:

- Micro-chipped.
- Vaccinated against rabies.
- Blood tested to confirm that the vaccine has taken effect at least six months before the animal is to return to the UK.
- Covered by a 'pet passport' to certify that these requirements have been met.

There is a statutory wait of at least 21 days after the final rabies vaccination before your pet can enter another EU country. Sweden and Malta have rules over and above the standard EU rules. It is advisable to contact the relevant authorities in your new country –the UK Embassy should be able to put you in touch - well in advance of relocation.

Only carriers authorised by the Department for Environment, Food and Rural Affairs (Defra) are allowed to carry pets. For a complete list of authorised carriers and further information on the 'pet passport' scheme, visit www.defra.gov.uk. This includes a list of contact details for Defra animal health divisional offices, which can also offer advice on transporting your pet abroad.

In the weeks before your departure, try to minimise the inevitable chaos you will experience in the immediate aftermath of moving abroad by letting relevant authorities and companies with whom you have dealings know of your change in address. The box on the previous page makes suggestions as to which people you may need to contact.

As with a move between properties within the UK, it pays to be systematic when recording what personal effects you need to move, and to keep detailed records of what is being sent and where it should go. This will not only help you ensure the removers put things in the right places when they arrive at the other end, but is useful in terms of insurance claims.

Your goods are likely to be transported in steel shipping containers, the two most common sizes of which are 20ft (which hold a volume of 30 cubic metres) and 40ft (which hold a volume of 65 cubic metres); they are large enough to include a car if required. A cheaper alternative is to send things in 'part load' or 'groupage'; this means that your consignment will be transported along with other consignments to the final destination.

Selling abroad

It may not be uppermost in your mind when you are buying, but it is useful to remember that at some point you may come to sell your overseas home. This chapter will provide useful information to help you do this correctly and efficiently.

Deciding to sell

In all the excitement of choosing, buying and using your property –
whether as a permanent home, somewhere for holidays or as a vehicle
to improve your finances – it can be easy to forget that at some point
you may come to sell.

There could be all sorts of reasons
why you decide to part company with
the overseas property that has become
so much a part of your life.

It may be that you have 'lived the
dream' of emigrating or owning a
second home and decided you have
had your fill of it. Illness or a family
crisis might have forced you to re-
evaluate your priorities and led you to
the conclusion that you should return
to the UK.

"It can be easy to forget that at some point you may have to sell."

You may simply have bought in one
country or area but have decided you
would prefer a different location. Or
you may be delighted with the
location but conclude that your
original choice of property is no longer
suitable, and so decide to look for
somewhere different.

If you bought as an investment,
you might now feel that the property
has served its financial purpose, and

that the capital tied up in it might
produce better returns if it were re-
invested somewhere else.

If you failed to do all your
calculations correctly in the first
place – or the lettings market just
did not turn out to be as favourable
as you had hoped – you may have
come to the conclusion that you
simply cannot afford to own the
property; or that you find the
generation of vital rental income too
stressful a task.

Whatever the reason, the net effect
is that you now face the long and
potentially time consuming prospect
of organising a sale.

GOING IT ALONE

In some countries estate agents'
commissions are much higher than in
the UK. You may already have
discovered this when you bought the
property, as it is possible you picked
up half the tab at that point – you
may even have paid a higher
percentage than you might expect to
pay as a seller in the UK.

If you cast your mind back to when
you bought the property, you may also

150

have experienced estate agency practices that differed hugely from what one might expect in the UK. You might have been subjected to extremely aggressive marketing by developers or their agents perhaps; you may have witnessed quite the opposite, finding it a challenge to even get hold of written details for a property, let alone plans or a decent quality photograph.

All this may have put you off using an estate agent altogether – and you would not be alone in that, because plenty of people overseas do go it alone rather than placing their properties with agencies. In some areas of Spain it is estimated that a fifth of all property transactions go through without an estate agent ever being involved, for example; in France a similar proportion sell their properties by 'having a word' with the local notary, or by putting up an 'a vendre' sign and placing adverts in the press.

If you are living on site rather than selling a property you only visit from time to time, such an approach may work well for you, and save you a substantial chunk of commission in the process. Your success or otherwise is likely to depend on how good a networker you are, and how much time and energy you are prepared to spend on doing your own marketing – putting the word around, taking up every available publicity opportunity and maybe even setting up a website and advertising this through friends back in the UK.

Think carefully about your own personal safety if you do go down this route, though – in no other situation would you put a sign up inviting complete strangers to come and look round your house. Make sure it is clear that viewings are by appointment only, and arrange for there to be more than one of you present at the property for every viewing.

Tips on selling without an agent

- Think carefully about how to present the property in its best light; be prepared to spend some of the commission you hope to save on ensuring the décor and furnishings look right
- Get a really good picture of local property prices by trawling through newspapers and staring in estate agents' windows
- If you can get a free or cheap valuation from one or more estate agent, do so
- Produce well-presented sales particulars describing the property, giving measurements and, if possible, high quality photography
- Be professional with all potential buyers and make sure the property is always clean and tidy

SELLING THROUGH AN AGENT

Especially if you are selling an overseas property from the UK, you are likely to want to have an estate agent's assistance. Even if it feels like an inconvenience, take the trouble to interview estate agents and 'host' their valuations in person – if only to get a good feel for whether you get on with them and how good they are with people – both of which are essential aspects of successful house selling. If an agent gets a sense that you cannot be bothered to make the effort to sell your own property, why on earth should he or she bother?

❝ Interview estate agents: try to get a feel for whether you get on with them and how good they are with people. ❞

When choosing between agents, always remember the following:

Check their credentials

As explained on page 58, it is important to feel confident that you are dealing with an estate agent you can trust so make sure that, where appropriate, they are fully licensed;

and that they are members of relevant professional bodies – which should mean they abide by a code of practice and could give you some degree of added protection if things go wrong.

Discuss their commission

Estate agents' fees vary significantly between countries, between regions and sometimes even between two local firms – as do conventions about whether the seller pays the whole commission or whether the cost is borne jointly with the buyer. For further details on typical commissions in the most popular countries among British buyers, see the table right and Chapter 8. It may be tempting to choose an agent purely on the basis of the commission he or she charges, but bear in mind that this may not be the best approach, as the quality of service you receive may be lower if you go for a cheap option. Remember also that commissions are always negotiable, so make it clear that you are shopping around for the best rate, rather than simply enquiring about the fee as if it is fixed in stone.

Clarify the marketing strategy

There are many different ways of marketing properties for sale, some more effective than others. In some countries, and especially in rural

 For information on checking an agent's credentials, see pages 58-61. Remember that the strength of regulation varies between countries.

Estate agents' commission – how rates vary

Country	Commission %	Comments
France	4-12	Generally paid by seller but in some areas buyer may have to pay half
Spain	6-10	Sellers often try to pass these costs on to buyers
Italy	6	Normally split 50/50 between buyer and seller (varies by region)
Portugal	5-10	Paid by the seller
Florida	6	Paid by seller
Cyprus	5+	Paid by seller
Turkey	6	Normally split 50/50 between buyer and seller
Bulgaria	3-10	Split 50/50 between buyer and seller
Czech Republic	3	Paid by seller
Poland	6	Split 50/50 between buyer and seller

(Illustration for comparison purposes only. Check with your agent for the actual rates applicable)

areas, advertising is very low-key – sometimes amounting to little more than a typed or even hand-written card in the window of an agency office in a small, far-from-bustling town. Particularly if you think your property is likely to appeal to a local audience, you may feel this kind of service is sufficient. But especially if you want to show the property to a wider market – including other overseas buyers – you are likely to want a more broad-ranging marketing strategy, involving web-based exposure and/or a link with a UK-based agency who will promote the

> **"** Any obvious deficiencies in a property will almost certainly lead potential buyers to push for a lower price. **"**

property through domestic channels. If an agent looks at you blankly at this point, move on.

Make sure you get on well

When you discuss marketing strategies with agents, you should feel like you and the agent are working in partnership to sell your property – rather than having the sense that they want to be left to do things in their own way, and that you are inconveniencing them by even wanting to know how they plan to earn their commission. To do their jobs effectively, estate agents need to be affable and charming people, with good selling skills. If they cannot achieve any of this with you, ask yourself how good they will be at persuading buyers that yours is the property of their dreams.

Check the contract

There are different ways of employing estate agents to work for you, and it is important to be happy with the arrangement you are entering into

before you sign any paperwork. Even in the UK, for example, estate agency contracts may refer to the agent being the 'sole selling agent' – this means they are the only agent with a right to sell your home, including you – so if you happened to sell the property yourself, you would still have to pay the agent. Under a 'sole agency' arrangement you would not have to pay the agent if you yourself found a buyer; under a 'multi-agency' deal more than one agency could be acting for you but you only have to pay the one that finally sells the property. Contracts can have lengthy tie-in periods, or can state that if anyone originally introduced by them buys the property – no matter if it is eighteen months later – they are still due a fee. These sorts of clauses can exist in foreign contracts too, so ask the agent for a contract to take away with you and have it checked over by your lawyer.

SETTING THE PRICE

There are numerous factors that are likely to influence the price your property can achieve, as shown in the diagram (right). You should be able to exert some level of control over some of these factors; others will be out of your hands.

 See page 102 for advice on the dangers of under-declaring the price of property. For rates of capital gains tax payable, see Chapter 8.

FACTORS AFFECTING HOUSE PRICES

The price of overseas properties is driven by a combination of factors. Some are local but others are linked to wider economic conditions.

Economic downturn in UK, leading to fewer overseas property buyers

Recession in country where property is, leading to fewer local buyers

Cost of borrowing increases, deterring buyers

Local over-supply of property depresses prices

Area was fashionable but is now 'old hat'

Property is poorly maintained and/or presented

UK economy in a boom, meaning plenty of overseas buyers

Native economy in a boom, leading to plenty of local buyers – whether looking for main or second homes

Cost of borrowing stable or heading downward

Shortage of good quality property in the local area

Area develops a particular cachet or 'up and coming' status

Property has the 'x' factor

Factors beyond your control

The overall state of the market – sometimes you happen to have to sell at a time when house prices are in freefall; it may be that you can hold on for a while until prices pick up, but you may not have that luxury. Equally, you may be lucky and be selling at a point where prices are stable or even heading in an upwards direction. Either way, this is down to macroeconomics rather than anything you individually can do much about (other than adjust your price accordingly).

The peculiarities of the local market – it may be that there are issues in your local area that could affect the ease or otherwise of you achieving a sale. Perhaps the local economy has taken a downturn, or a major employer has moved out of the area, reducing housing demand; maybe there has been so much investment in construction that there is now an over-supply of property relative to local demand?

Factors you can influence

How quickly you need to sell – with the best will in the world it is not always possible to plan for every eventuality, and there is always the possibility that for personal or family reasons you find yourself needing to sell more quickly than you might have expected. But if you have followed our advice on planning your purchase carefully in advance, you will hopefully not find yourself in the position of needing to sell in a hurry for financial reasons, at least. The less time pressure you are under when selling, the less likely you are to end up taking a lower price than you might otherwise have achieved.

Problems with your property – sometimes what limits the price a property can command is the kind of structural or decorative issues that cost money, time and organisational effort, like leaky roofs, windows in need of replacement or poor quality rendering. Other problems like rights of way issues or boundary disputes – even if you have had no difficulties because of them since buying – will almost certainly come back to haunt you, so if you have any way of sorting out such problems before selling, it is normally advisable to do so. Any obvious deficiencies in a property will almost certainly lead potential buyers to push for a lower price, and may be enough to put them off altogether.

Whether or not your property has the 'x' factor – a well chosen property, sympathetically presented and with the right mixture of neutral practicality and imaginative personal touches will achieve the best possible price whatever the prevailing market is doing. The 'x' factor may not be easy to define, but plenty of buyers know it when they see it, and are prepared to pay extra too.

Places to buy

The range of countries popular among UK property hunters is vast and growing. From here until the end of the book, we provide key details of how to buy and settle in the most appealing locations.

France

Go for village houses or farm buildings to renovate; or city, ski and beach apartments with letting potential.

The property market

The most popular areas in France for British property buyers have tended to be to the north and west of the country, from Brittany and Normandy down through the Loire Valley, to the Dordogne region. More recently the south of the country has opened up to British buyers thanks to a plethora of budget air routes, with areas around Bordeaux, Toulouse, the Pyrenees and Languedoc-Roussillon attracting many second home owners and retirees. Paris, the Côte d'Azur and the Alps are perennial favourites offering reliable tourist rental income. Newer areas for buyers wanting rural renovation properties include inland regions such as Limousin and Auvergne.

How to buy

The *compromis de vente* (preliminary contract) commits both parties to the transaction and on signing you must pay a deposit of around 10%, which you forfeit if you default; the seller must pay you twice as much if they pull out. Because you commit to the sale so early in the process, your lawyer must negotiate appropriate *conditions suspensives* ('get out' clauses), to allow you to walk away from the deal under pre-defined circumstances – for example if it turns out that there are rights of way which would reduce your enjoyment of the property.

If you buy an unfinished property you will need to sign a *contrat de réservation*. There are strict rules about the staging of payments as the building progresses. Your lawyer should push for an 'extrinsic' guarantee, through which a bank or insurer pledges to complete the development if the developer goes bust (see page 83).

If you are planning a renovation project, the *certificat d'urbanisme* is a vital document. There are two types – the *certificat de simple information*, which tells you whether the existing property meets required building standards and has any valid planning permissions; and the *certificat opérationelle*, which tells you whether your planned changes or extensions will be allowed. You will need an architect or surveyor to apply for the *certificat*, and should make the purchase conditional on receiving a positive response from the *mairie* (town hall).

The final stage of the buying process is the signing of the *acte de vente* (deed of sale), which must be done in the presence of a *notaire* (notary).

The 'leaseback' model of property investment was pioneered in France, under the government-backed *Residence de Tourisme* initiative to encourage investment in tourist infrastructure. Benefits include VAT reimbursement, although the relevant

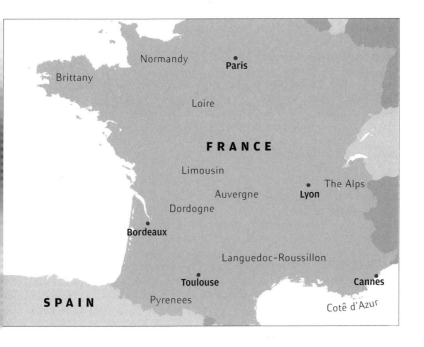

proportion must be repaid if you sell within 20 years. Leasebacks are now offered by developers in many parts of France; leases generally last nine years, but the developer may retain a right to renew. Have your lawyer check any deals thoroughly.

Fees and taxes

- **Estate agents' commission** – varies from 4% to 12%; generally paid by the seller but in some areas buyer may have to pay half. Details should be set out in the agent's *mandat* (letter of authority to sell) from the seller
- **Stamp duty** – *droits d'enregistrement* for properties over five years old: 4.8%
- **VAT** – *taxe sur la valeur ajoutée* (TVA) on new properties: 19.6%
- **Mortgage/registration fees** – to register lender's first charge against property, 1-2%; for arrangement of loan, 1%

- **Notaries' fees** – allow 1–2%
- **Council taxes** – *taxe foncière* (land tax), based on property's theoretical rentable value (this can be waived for two years if recently renovated); *taxe d'habitation* (occupancy tax), paid by whoever is resident on January 1 (exemptions are possible while property is uninhabitable, and retirees may be eligible for a reduced rate); *ordures* (rubbish tax).

Red tape

Before you buy a French property you must have an INSEE (*Institut National de la Statistique et des Études Économiques*) number, obtainable from the local tax office.

After three months, you may apply for a *carte de séjour* (residence permit), obtainable from the local *préfecture de police* (administrative centre for policing and legal matters); the *carte* can be useful when applying for other permits, for example a driving licence, although having one is no longer compulsory for UK citizens.

The French tax system is complicated, and there are many different ways of handling both the purchase and your ongoing liabilities, which will include *impôt sur le revenu* (income tax) on rentals and *droits de succession* (inheritance tax).

French income tax is a progressive tax with the different rates being applied to the net salary after social security contributions. There are a wide range of rebates and exemptions granted on gross income which allow a more moderate rate of taxation. Families in France benefit from a system known as *le quotient familial* (family quota), through which their taxable income is divided into units reflecting the family status of the tax-payer.

For example, people living alone represent one unit and are taxed on the whole of their income. A married couple are considered as two units and their joint income will be divided by two. In addition, the first two children count as one-half a unit each and each additional child is counted as a full unit – so the more children you have, the lower your tax liability.

Capital gains tax – *plus value* – is charged at 16% of the net gain. As a French resident you pay an extra 10% in French National Insurance, making the effective rate 26%. As a non-French resident you may be exempt from *plus value* if you have lived in the property and been French tax resident for two years at some point (even if not at the point of sale). People in receipt of state pension may also be exempt.

Particular issues you may need to discuss with your legal/tax adviser include: your matrimonial regime; whether to rent the property furnished or unfurnished; whether or not to define yourself as a professional landlord; and whether to buy through a *société civile immobilière* (a sort of company you can set up, through which you buy the property).

Inheritance tax is a particular problem, because there is no exemption for spouses and nil rate bands are much less generous than in the UK. Rates can be as high as 60%. Both married and unmarried couples need to plan their approach to purchasing carefully in advance.

For more information on French tax, get in touch with a specialist tax adviser; for basic information contact the French Embassy in London (see web address below), or your local tax office if in France.

Health and social security

If you are moving to France you should register with your local *Caisse Primaire d'Assurance Maladie* office and provide them with any forms you have in respect of the reciprocal healthcare agreements between the UK and the other EEA countries, such as an E106 or E121, which will exempt you from paying French social security contributions. To find your local CPAM visit www.ameli.fr (French) and find the office for your *département* using the designated search facility.

If you are working in salaried employment or earning a reasonable amount through self-employment you must, after 12 months, start to contribute to the French Social Security scheme. If you are not working or on a low income and have been resident in France for longer than 3 months, you can apply to be covered by *Couverture Maladie Universelle* (universal health cover), which is designed to ensure that everyone is covered for basic medical costs. It is not available to people already compulsorily insured under another scheme.

Under the CMU system, you have to pay the majority of healthcare providers up-front and then be reimbursed. The French Social Security defines the cost of virtually every type of medical treatment using the *Tarif de Convention* (official or conventional rate) and reimburses medical expenses at an average of 70% of this rate – if the doctor you visit is *conventionne* (which means they charge in accordance with the tariff).

The level of reimbursement depends on two factors – the nature of the treatment and its cost; and the level of income of you and your family – so until you have filled in your first year's French tax return you will be covered by your E106.

Most people take out what is known as a 'top-up' policy (*complémentaire* or *mutuelle*) to cover the gap between what the state provides and the amount charged. Low income families, including expatriates, may be eligible for free top-up policies. With many policies you will be given a *carte blanche* (top-up insurance card), through which your treatment will be recorded and the appropriate balance reimbursed.

In France, as in any other foreign country, think carefully about health costs, and consider taking out private health cover. If you have a second home in France, ensure you have a European Health Insurance Card and take out a comprehensive travel insurance policy to cover you and your family whenever you visit.

France

Other public services

- To find contact information for your local French town hall – which can provide information on a huge variety of aspects of French life, from education to planning permission, visit the *Mairies de France* website, www.mairiesdefrance.org.
- For information about the national education system, contact the *Ministère de L'Education Nationale* via www.education.gouv.fr. Comprehensive information is also available from Eurydice, the information network on education in Europe, via www.eurydice.org/Eurybase/ frameset_eurybase.html. To find out about private schools, contact the *Centre d'information et de documentation de l'enseignement privé* via its website, www.enseignement-prive.info/ (French). You may also want to contact COBISEC, the council of British international schools, on 01367 242655 or via www.cobisec.org. The British Embassy in France holds lists of English-speaking schools by region.
- For information about recognition of UK qualifications in France, visit the Europe Open for Professions website at www.dfes.gov.uk/europeopen/index.shtml and follow the links; alternatively contact

the European Network of national Information Centres on academic recognition and qualifications, via www.enic-naric.net/.

Finding professionals

- The British Embassy in France can help you find English-speaking lawyers, as well as providing a range of other advice and services. Contact details are listed on the website, which is accessible via www.britishembassy.gov.uk.
- The Franco-British Chamber of Commerce and Industry has a directory of members working in a variety of fields, including accountancy, building professions and translating; it can also provide help and advice if you want to set up in business. Visit www.francobritishchambers.com.
- Estate agents should be members of the *Fédération Nationale des Agents Immobiliers et Mandataires* (www.fnaim.fr), the *Syndicat Nationales des Professionels Immobilier* (www.snpi.com) or the *Union Nationale de l'Immobilier* (www.unit.fr).

- To find a surveyor, search the Royal Institution of Chartered Surveyors' directory via www.ricsfirms.co.uk/.
- To find an *expert immobilier*, search by location on the online database of the *Chambre des Experts Immobiliers*, whose website is at www.experts-fnaim.org.
- Possible sources of architects include the Royal Institute of British Architects (www.riba.org); the *Conseil National de l'Ordre des Architectes* (www.architectes.org); the *Syndicat d'Architecture* (www.syndarch.com) and the *Union Nationale des Syndicats Français d'Architectes* (www.unsfa.com).
- The British Embassy in France holds lists of certified translators/interpreters; alternatively you could search the online database of the Institute of Linguists, at www.iol.org.uk.

Utility companies

- Electricity and gas provision is nationalised. For electricity contact the local office of *Electricité de France* via +08 10 12 61 26 or visit http://particuliers.edf.fr. For gas call +08 10 14 01 50 or visit www.gazdefrance.com.
- For water and rubbish collection services, contact your local town hall to find your

designated providers.
- To have a telephone line installed or changed into your name, contact *France Télécom* on +08 92 70 57 04 or 1004.
- If you own a TV, you must pay the *redevance audiovisuelle* (annual TV) licence, which is normally added to your annual *taxe d'habitation* bill.

Miscellaneous resources

- The website of the French Embassy in London, www.ambafrance-uk.org, has

information about many aspects of French life.

- The BBC runs an online French language course, and courses based on the TV and web. Visit www.bbc.co.uk/languages to find out more. To find a French course near you, try the BBC's language course search facility, provided in association with Learn Direct, at www.bbc.co.uk/learning/coursesearch/languages/.

There are a host of resources of interest to British people living, considering living, or just owning property in France. These include:

- Expat.Telegraph – the wide-ranging expatriate news and advice service from the Daily Telegraph, available online at www.expat.telegraph.co.uk.
- Expatica – useful background information on life in France, available online at www.expatica.com
- Lost In France – online guide, featuring a range of resources including forums and listings, available at www.lost-in-france.com
- French Entrée – comprehensive site featuring fact sheets, case studies and advice columns relating to property and life in France, available at www.frenchentree.com.
- Living France – monthly magazine about all aspects of living in/moving to France, available in newsagents and by subscription via 01858 438832, or online at www.livingfrance.com.
- The British Embassy in France publishes lists of relevant expat organisations and English-language publications by region.

Tourism/travel information

- French Tourist Board: www.franceguide.com, www.francetourism.com
- For information about services operating through the Channel Tunnel, visit www.eurotunnel.com or phone 08705 35 35 35
- Ferry companies operating to French ports: P&O (www.poferries.com); Sea France (www.seafrance.com); Southern Ferries (www.sncm.fr); Brittany Ferries (www.brittany ferries.com); Condor Ferries (www.condorferries.co.uk); Hover Speed (www.hoverspeed.co.uk); Norfolk Line (www.norfolkline.com); Speed Ferries (www.speed ferries.com).
- For information about French motorways: www.autoroutes.fr
- For information about trains: www.sncf.fr
- Eurolines operates scheduled coach services to many French destinations from London, with regional connections by National Express. Visit www.gobycoach.com
- French national airline: Air France, www.airfrance.com

163

Spain

As well as properties along every inch of coastline, rural and urban properties inland are growing in popularity.

The property market

Overseas property buyers have had a love affair with the three main Spanish coastal strips – the Costa del Sol, Costa Blanca and Costa Brava – for the last three decades. In recent years developers have been opening up new stretches of coast, including the Costa de Almeria, Costa de la Luz and Costa del Azahar; others have started to head inland, creating golfing complexes and even spa resorts. Some buyers are attracted to Spain's cities, including Barcelona, Valencia, Seville and Madrid, and there is a growing tendency to explore the country's undiscovered interior. Spain's islands – the Balearics and Canaries – are popular choices for British and northern European buyers.

How to buy

The *contrato privado de compraventa* (preliminary contract) commits the seller to sell the property to you at the agreed price, and commits you to buy. As in France it is essential to negotiate conditions under which you are able to pull out of the deal, by way of inserting *condiciones resolutorias* (escape clauses) into the contract. You will generally pay a 10% deposit at this point.

You may have been advised by your estate agent to make an offer to buy, whereby you would pay an *arras* (deposit) of around 2–5% of the purchase price and promise to complete the transaction within a set period – but lawyers advise moving straight to a properly negotiated *contrato privado* instead.

If you are buying off-plan you may be asked to pay a substantial deposit on agreeing a reservation contract; your lawyer should negotiate for a clear and reasonable schedule of stage payments, as well as ensuring there is an appropriate guarantee in place, to cover you in case the developer goes bust or is otherwise unable to complete the project. An alternative approach, sometimes used where you buy from a small Spanish builder, is to buy the land outright and whatever has been built on it already, and enter into a separate contract for building the rest of the property.

If you are buying in a villa or apartment complex, you will almost certainly be buying into a *comunidad de propietarios* (community of owners), which looks after communal swimming pools, lifts, gardens and the like. Check its *reglementos* (rules) carefully.

The *escritura de compraventa* (deed of sale) is the document that legally transfers the property into your ownership. It must be signed in the presence of a *notario* (notary), who will register it in the *registro de la propiedad* (property register) and *registro catastral* (tax register).

Self-build is popular in Spain and can be cheaper than renovation, but make sure

any land you buy is zoned in such a way that you are allowed to build on it.

Take extreme caution if you are looking to buy in the autonomous region of Valencia, where a law passed in 1994 means that all land may be converted for property development, unless it has been deemed not 'urbanizable' on historical, cultural or ecological grounds.

This means that *suelo rústico* (rural land) may be re-designated as fit for property development if the town hall approves a developer's plan for such change of use – a developer may therefore compulsorily purchase some or all of your land (and whatever you have built on it), often at prices well below market value. Land classed as 'urbanizable' can also be affected; and even land already classified as urban can, in some cases, be affected by future developments. This law is currently under review both within Spain and at European level (see miscellaneous resources section for website details).

Fees and taxes

- **Estate agents' fees** – can range between 6% and 10%, and sellers often try to pass these costs on to buyers; clarify what fee is due in your initial discussions
- **VAT** – *impuesto sobre el valor anadido*

(IVA) is payable at 7% on new-builds and self-builds
- **Property transfer tax** – *impuesto sobre transmisiones patrimonial* is charged at 6% on all other purchases
- **Stamp duty** – 0.5% on new-builds

165

- **Notary fees** – allow 0.5 to 1%
- **Local capital gains tax** – *plus valia* or *impuesto sobre el incremento del valor de los terrenos de naturaleza urbana* – is levied on sellers, but by convention is paid by the buyer (because the bill will arrive after the sale goes through, by which point the seller has disappeared anyway). The tax is calculated on a progressive scale from 2 to 40%, and is only likely to be costly if the property has not been sold for a long time and its value has shot up – the best advice is to contact the town hall to find out what is due, and try to negotiate the equivalent amount off the price
- **Withholding tax** – if you buy from a non-Spanish resident (who has owned the property for less than ten years), you must pay 5% of the purchase price direct to the taxman rather than to the seller; this amount is then offset against the seller's capital gains tax liability.

Red tape

In advance of signing the deeds to buy a property in Spain you will need a *numero de indentidad de extranjero* (NIE number). If you are in Spain you must go in person to the nearest *oficina de extranjeros* (immigration office) or *comisarias de policia nacional* (police station), with your passport, some passport photos, a copy of the house purchase contract and a completed form. If you are in the UK you can apply through the Spanish consulates in London, Manchester and Edinburgh.

If you are planning to live in Spain for more than three months, you should apply to the same office for a *targeta de residencia* (residence permit); these can be temporary (for up to one year) or permanent (for five years, automatically renewable). Strictly speaking this is not obligatory if you are employed, self-employed or a student, but it can make life easier when applying for other permits, dealing with utility companies and the like.

Tax-wise if you are renting your property out you will be liable for *impuesto sobre la renta de no residentes* (income tax on rentals), which for non-residents is charged at a flat rate of 25% of gross rents. It can in some circumstances, if your rental earnings are high enough, be worthwhile to set up as a business in order to claim back reliefs and allowances.

Even if you do not rent it out, if your property is a second home the Spanish authorities will tax you as if you do – they calculate a notional income based on 2% of the declared value of the property (or 1% if the *valor catastral* (rateable value) has been revalued since 1994), and tax this at 25%.

Council taxes – *impuesto sobre bienes immuebles* – must be paid by whoever occupies the property on January 1 (you or your tenant if you are letting the property out on a permanent basis); you will also be liable for *basura* (refuse tax) and other one-off taxes raised by town halls.

When you file your tax return for income tax you will also be assessed for *patrimonio* (wealth tax), which residents and non-residents must pay on their total assets in Spain (minus any Spanish mortgages), on a progressive scale from 0.2% to 2.5%.

If you sell your property you will be liable for capital gains tax – charged at 15% if you are a Spanish resident, 35% if non-resident; although allowances may reduce your liability after about five years of ownership.

As in France it is particularly important in Spain to discuss whose name should go on the deeds and, if appropriate, to define your matrimonial regime – this can help minimise your heirs' inheritance tax liabilities. Inheritance tax in Spain is calculated on a progressive scale, and the taxman imposes multipliers to these according to the 'closeness' of the person inheriting, and their overall pre-existing wealth; there is no exemption even for spouses.

The Spanish Finance Ministry publishes a book in English called 'Taxation Regulations for Foreigners'; see also the website of the *Agencia Tributaria* (equivalent of the Inland Revenue) at www.aeat.es.

Healthcare

If you live and work in Spain you must pay into the Spanish Social Security system. First you will need to get a social security number card from the local *Tesorería de Seguridad Social*, which you then present at the local *ambulatorio* (outpatients clinic/ walk-in medical centre) and fill in a form for a *tarjeta sanitaria* (health card).

Public health benefits under the national health system (*Instituto Nacional de la Salud*) include general and specialist medical care, hospitalisation, laboratory services, discounted drugs and medicines, basic dental care, maternity care, appliances and transportation. But note that social security covers only around 75% of the cost of treatment. Completely free treatment is available only in certain hospitals, where waiting lists are very long. For the non-reimbursed costs you will almost certainly want to set up supplementary insurance.

Bear in mind that not all doctors work for the state system. For more information visit www.ingesa.msc.es.

As a UK pensioner living in Spain you will be entitled to receive free medical treatment under the same conditions as Spanish state pensioners, provided you obtain form E121 from the DSS in the UK and take this to the local *Oficina del Instituto Nacional de Seguridad Social* – along with your residence card (or application form for it) and passport. You will receive a *tarjeta de afiliación* card and be assigned to an *ambulatorio*. Prescribed medicines are free for pensioners.

If you have a second home in Spain, ensure you have a European Health Insurance Card and take out a comprehensive travel insurance policy to cover you and your family whenever you visit.

Other public services

- If you are a UK state pensioner you can have your pension paid in Spain; more generally as a Spanish resident your social security rights are the same as Spaniards'. The Spanish system of social security is administered by the *Instituto Nacional de la Seguridad Social* (INSS). Benefits cover healthcare, sickness, pensions, unemployment and invalidity. For further information on all benefits

whilst in Spain contact your local office of the INSS or the head office on tel 00 34 91 5688300.
- Education is obligatory for all children aged 6-16 if the parents are legally resident in Spain, and is free from pre-school to 18 years. Pre-school is not obligatory, so the same is not true of under-6s. The availability of places depends on the area of Spain and

167

demand for them. The Spanish Ministry of Education and Science is at www.mec.es.

The British Council has details of schools in Spain which offer an English-type education. Most are members of the National Association of British Schools in Spain, which organises periodic inspections by British inspectors. For further details, visit www.britishcouncil.org.uk/spain.

- For information about procedures in Spain for confirming equivalence of qualifications, contact the *Subdirección General de Títulos, Convalidaciones y Homologaciones* at wwwn.mec.es or follow the links on the Europe Open for Professions website at www.dfes.gov.uk; alternatively contact the European Network of national information centres on academic recognition and qualifications, via www.enic-naric.net/.

Finding professionals

- The British Embassy in Spain can help you find English-speaking lawyers, as well as providing a range of other advice and services. Contact details are listed on the website, which is accessible via www.britishembassy. gov.uk.
- The British Chamber of Commerce in Spain has a directory of members working in a variety of fields, including accountancy, building professions and translating; it can also provide help and advice if you want to set up in business and even advertises a small number of job vacancies. Visit www.britishchamber spain.com.
- Estate agents should be members of the *Gestores Intermediarios en Promociones de Edificaciones* (www.gipe.es – Spanish) or the *Agentes de la Propiedad*

Inmobiliaria (www.consejocoapis.org – Spanish).
- To find a surveyor, search the Royal Institution of Chartered Surveyors' directory via www.ricsfirms.co.uk/.
- Possible sources of architects include the Royal Institute of British Architects (www.riba.org) and the *Consejo Superior de los Colegios de Arquitectos de Espana* (www.cscae.com).
- If you have problems finding a *gestor*, or want to check that your *gestor* is fully qualified and certified, contact your local *gestors' college*, which you can find via the *Consejo General de los Colegios de Gestores Administrativos* at http://consejo. gestores.net/colegio_profesion.htm.

Utility companies

- Your utility providers will vary according to where your property is located. If you have a new electricity connection be prepared to provide documentation such as a *boletin de enganche* (connection certificate), supplied by the electrician who installed your wiring, and a *Licencia de Primera ocupación* (first occupation licence), available from the town hall.

Otherwise you will probably carry on the existing supply, although even this will require you to provide paperwork like the title deed of the property in your name.
- To set up a contract for the supply of gas bottles you may need to have the property inspected.
- Your water will usually be supplied by a company which has a contract with the

local council, so if in doubt contact the town hall – again, proof of ownership and identity will be required, and an official water installation certificate (*boletin del agua*) if the property is new. In the case of a property which is part of a *communidad*, there may also be payments to be made to a further company for the maintenance of a community well.

- The main telephone company in Spain is *Telefonica*, although there are other companies in telecoms. Connection and transfer fees are similar to those in the UK. Dial 1004 or visit www.telefonica.es.
- There is no TV licence in Spain.

Miscellaneous resources

- For general advice on buying and owning property in Spain, you may wish to contact the Institute of Foreign Property Owners (*Instituto de Propietarios Extranjeros*), Conde de Altea 33, 03590 Altea (Calpe), tel: + 95 584 32 12, or the Association of Spanish Property Owners, West Heath House, 32 North End Road, London NW11 7PT.
- The Spanish Embassy Office for Economic and Commercial Affairs has a website at http://www.mcx.es/londres.
- The BBC runs an online Spanish language course, and courses based on the TV and web. Visit www.bbc.co.uk/languages to find out more. To find a Spanish course near you, try the BBC's language course search facility, provided in association with Learn Direct, at www.bbc.co.uk/learning/coursesearch/languages/.
- For information about Spanish courses in the UK, visit the UK site of the Spanish Ministry of Education and Science, at http://www.sgci.mec.es/uk/english.html.
- The British Embassy in Spain can provide a list of English-speaking organisations
- For information about the Valencia land grab, visit www.abusos-no.org.

Other resources for expatriates include:
- Expat.Telegraph – the wide-ranging expatriate news and advice service from the Daily Telegraph, available online at www.expat.telegraph.co.uk.
- Expatica – useful background information on life in Spain, available online at www.expatica.com
- Spain Expat – online expatriate information resources, with links to other expat resources, available at www.spainexpat.com.

To get a flavour of Spain before moving to, or looking for property in, Spain:
- Spain Magazine, published monthly – available in newsagents and on subscription, tel 0131 226 7766 or visit www.spainmagazine.co.uk for more details.
- Living Spain magazine, published monthly – available in newsagents and on subscription, tel 01283 742970 or visit www.livingspain. co.uk for more details.
- The official site of the Spanish Tourist Board is at www.spain.info.
- Spanish national airline: Iberia, www.iberia.com.
- Ferries to Santander and Bilbao are available from P&O (www.poferries. com) and Brittany Ferries (www.brittanyferries.com).
- For information about trains: http://horarios.renfe.es/hir/ingles.html.

Italy

Most foreign buyers opt for hilltop seclusion, but city and coastal property is also on the way up.

The property market

For many years Tuscany has been the most popular region among British house buyers. Umbria to the south east and Le Marche further to the east also offer plenty of potential, and more recently markets in more southerly, coastal regions such as Puglia and Calabria have opened up. To the north, the Ligurian coast is popular with wealthy Italians, and some British buyers have also ventured into the northern Italian Lakes. Rome, Venice and Florence have year-round tourist appeal but property prices are high. Sardinia and Sicily are growing in popularity.

How to buy

Once you have found a property you wish to buy, the first step towards securing it is to make a written offer, called a *proposta d'acquisto irrevocabile* – which is binding for up to 15 days. If you are buying a new-build property, especially through a developer, you may have to make a '*prenotazione*' booking. Either way, you may need to pay a small goodwill deposit at this point, but make sure the documentation clarifies that this is an *acconto*, meaning the money is returnable if the purchase does not go ahead.

The preliminary purchase contract or *compromesso* sets out the terms of the deal, and on signing you must pay a deposit of up to a third of the purchase price. There are two types of deposit – a *caparra confirmatoria* (if you decide not to buy, you lose the deposit and the seller can take you to court to complete the transaction; if the seller pulls out they must pay you twice the deposit and you have a similar right to force the sale); and a *caparra penitenziale* (similar but where neither party has legal recourse to force the deal).

The public sale contract, whereby title to the property is officially transferred to you, is called the *rogito* or *atto pubblico di compravendita*, which must be administered by a notary (*notaio*).

Fees and taxes

- **Estate agents' commission** – *provvigione*: around 3% each from buyer and seller (varies by region)
- **Registration tax** – *imposta di registro*: 7%
- **Stamp duties** – *imposta ipotecaria*, 2%; *imposta catastale*, 1%
- **For properties in rural register**, total registration/transfer taxes: 18%

(In all cases, rates are reduced to around 3–4% in total if the property is to be your main home (*prima casa*) for at least the next five years, and you take up residence within 18 months of buying)

- **VAT** – *imposta sul valore aggiunto* (IVA): 10% if bought new from a builder/developer; 4% if it will be your *prima casa*; 20% if it is designated as deluxe (*di lusso*). If IVA applies, other purchase taxes are reduced to nominal fees.
- **Notaries' fees**: fixed in bands by law; typical fee for 100,000 euro property, 1.5%
- **Council tax** – *imposta comunale immobili*: charged at 4–6% of the land registry value (*valore catastale*). There are separate taxes for rubbish disposal (*nettezza urbana*) and water (*acquedotto comunale*).

Red tape

In order to buy an Italian property you must first have a *codice fiscale* (equivalent to a National Insurance number), obtainable from the local tax office (*ufficio imposte diretto*) – look in the telephone directory under '*Uffici Finanzia*'.

The pre-purchase searches may be handled by a *geometra* – an independent professional who is a cross between an architect and a surveyor – or a lawyer (*avvocato*); the *notaio* will also conduct searches but does not owe you a duty of care. If you use a *geometra*, he or she can also handle any planning applications if you are buying a property that needs restoration.

If you buy land or property that is designated as rural, you must clarify whether anyone has pre-emption rights – neighbours who are farmers have first refusal when agricultural land comes on the market, so your representative must inform them and give them 30 days to make a formal declaration that they do or do not wish to take up the option. If you fail to do this, they have up to one year from the date of the sale to exercise their rights.

If you plan to live and work in Italy, you will be liable for income tax (*imposta sul reddito delle persone fisiche*) and may want to employ a book-keeper (*ragioniere*) or accountant (*commercialista*) to handle your tax affairs.

Non-Italian residents must pay income tax on rental income (minus relevant costs, for example for repairs or management expenses) – the rate is likely to be around 30%. You must also pay an income tax on the notional rental value of your house, even if you do not actually rent it out. This

171

is based on the official *rendita catastrale* (rateable value) and is normally small. Capital gains are taxed as income if you sell within five years. There is no inheritance tax in Italy.

If you plan to live and work in Italy you must report to the local police headquarters (*questura*) to apply for a residence permit (*permesso di soggiorno*); you may also need a work permit (*libretto di lavoro*). Contact your nearest Italian consulate or the local chamber of commerce. www.chamberofcommerce.it lists contact details for every chamber in Italy.

Health and social security

Once you have a residence permit, you can register with your local health authority (*unita sanitaria locale*) to obtain your national health number. You can then register with a doctor (*medico convenzionato*) The British Embassy has contact details for English-speaking doctors if you prefer to pay privately for one.

The Italian national health system (*Servizio Sanitario Nazionale*) offers low-cost health care of a good standard, with well-trained and dedicated doctors, though waiting lists can be long. The top private hospitals rival those of any country. State hospitals vary in quality, hence the popularity of private health insurance. As an employed or self-employed person living in Italy you will need to pay Italian national insurance to the *Instituto National Di Previdenza Sociale*, www.inps.it.

Other public services

- For European-wide information on education, social security and tax regimes, visit: www.eurydice.org.
- To find out about equivalence of academic qualifications, contact the Centro Informazione Mobilita Equivalenze Accademiche, via www.cimea.it.

- The Italian government's website, with links to individual departments, is at www.italia.gov.it.
- *Ministero degli Affari Esteri* (Italian Ministry of Foreign Affairs), tel: +39 06.3691.8899, www.esteri.it, email relazioni.pubblico@esteri.it

Language courses

- The BBC runs an online Italian language course, and courses based on the TV and web. Visit www.bbc.co.uk/languages to find out more. To find an Italian course near you, try the BBC's language course search facility, provided in association with Learn Direct, at www.bbc.co.uk/learning/coursesearch/languages/.

- Other language course providers include Training Club, www.training club.com; and the *Societa Dante Alighieri*, www.ladante.it.
- The Italian state TV channel, RAI, offers a free online Italian course via www.educational.rai.it/ioparloitaliano/

172

Finding professionals

- The British Embassy lists English-speaking lawyers, doctors and dentists in Italy at www.britishembassy.gov.uk.
- Try looking in Italian Yellow Pages, which is available online at www.paginegialle.it. Or the British Chamber of Commerce in Italy, www.britchamitaly.com.
- Check if your estate agent is a member of the *Federazione Italiana degli Agenti Immobiliari Professionali* or the *Federazione Italiana dei Mediatori e Agenti in Affari*, which are contactable via www.fiaip.it and www.fimaa.it.

- *Avvocati* should be verifiable through their national representative body, whose website is www.albonazionaleavvocati.it/; the equivalent body for notaries is www.notariato.it.
- Translators may be listed with the national association of translators and interpreters, contactable via www.aiti.org.
- The national body for *geometri* has a website at www.cng.it; the national body for *commercialisti* is at www.cndc.it.
- To find contact details of the relevant local council, visit www.comuni-italiani.it.

Utility companies

- For electricity and gas, contact *Enel* via www.enel.it or tel (from Italy) 800 900 800
- For water, contact your local *comune*.
- For telephones, contact *Telecom Italia* on tel. +39 06 3688 (from Italy dial 187)

or www.telecomitalia.it. Other providers include *Wind*, tel +39 06 83111(from Italy dial 155) or www.wind.it; and *Albacom*, tel +39 02 752921 (from Italy dial 195) or www.albacom.it.

General information sources

- The British Embassy in Rome, tel. (+39) 06 4220 0001, www.britain.it
- Italian press: Corriere della Sera, visit www.corriere.it; Repubblica, visit www.repubblica.it; Panorama magazine, www.panorama.it
- To open a bank account, if you are not a permanent resident, approach an Italian bank with offices in the UK, like the *Banca Commerciale Italiana* or *Banca di Roma*. The UK office will liaise with a local branch in Italy. Another option is to use a *BancoPosta* service offered by Italian Post Offices; further information at www.poste.it/bancoposta.
- The Informer – business, cultural and community information, including

universities and international schools, online at www.informer.it
- Expats In Italy – information and advice from people who have moved to Italy, online at www.expatsinitaly.com.
- What's On in Rome – English language guide at www.whatsoninrome.com
- Easy Milano – articles on life in Milan and Italy, online at www.easymilano.it.
- The Florentine – features and listings for Florence and surrounding area; online at www.theflorentine.net.
- Italian State Tourist Board: www.enit.it
- Italian Touring Club: www.touringclub.it
- National parks across Italy: www.parks.it
- Train timetables: www.trenitaliaplus.com
- Italian national airline: www.alitalia.it

Portugal

The Algarve is a golfer's paradise, but countryside and coasts to the north can offer bargains.

The property market

The Algarve, popular with British tourists since the 1970s, is by far the most common choice for second home hunters and retirees alike. Holiday rental yields and build quality are considered good. Many people opt for properties close to, or on, golf course complexes. The Portuguese capital Lisbon and its nearby Estoril coast have well-established tourist infrastructures; further north, new motorway connections ensure that the Costa de Prata (Silver Coast) and the Costa Verde (Green Coast) towards Oporto are making their mark with British buyers too.

How to buy

Both parties must agree a promissory contract (*contrato de promessa de compra e venda*) detailing the conditions of sale; this is legally binding on both sides and the law requires the seller to repay twice the deposit (which could be from 10 to 30% of the purchase price) should he or she withdraw from the sale.

It is important for your lawyer to ensure that any plans held by the local council (*camara municipal*) referring specifically to the property agree with the existing construction; they should also confirm any details about planning permission and plans for future construction nearby. The property must have a habitation licence (*licenca de habitual*), a *certidao do registo predial* (title deed) and a detailed *caderneta urbana* or *caderneta rustica* from the tax office – which acts like an ID card for the property.

The formal transfer of the property takes place at the signing of the *escritura de compra e venda*, in front of a *notano* (notary); registration at the *Conservatória do Registo Predial* should take place as soon as possible afterwards.

Fees and taxes

- **Estate agents' commission** – generally from 5 to 10%, paid by the seller
- **Legal fees** – allow around 4–5% to pay for your lawyer, *notano* and land registry fees.
- **Transfer tax** – *imposto municipal sobre as transmissoes*, which is charged on the market value of the property, on a sliding scale from 0–8% according to the value of the property – it is best to allow around 5–6%. Land for building is charged at a flat rate of 6.5% and

property owned through offshore companies (an old way of buying to avoid SISA tax, which no longer exists), at 15%.

- **Council taxes** – *imposto municipal sobre imoveis*, which is levied at different rates according to the value and age of the property. Allow 0.2 to 0.5% of rateable value for a new property and 0.4 to 0.8% for an old property. The introduction of this tax – a replacement for the old *contribuicao autarquica*, which was charged at between 0.8% and 1.3% but often calculated on ludicrously low declared values – is part of Portugal's attempt to wage war on under-declaration of property values, so do not take the value on the previous title deed as the starting point.

Red tape

Before you buy a property in Portugal, you will need to obtain a *numero de contribuente* (fiscal number) from the local tax office (*finanças*).

If you are planning to settle in Portugal you must apply for a residence permit from the nearest office of the Portuguese Immigration Service – *Serviço de Estrangeiros e Fronteiras* – the contact details of which you can find through the main SEF website at www.sef.pt/, along with copies of the necessary application forms.

As a non-resident you are liable for income tax on rental income, which will be charged according to a progressive scale (top rate 40%) depending on your overall income in Portugal. If you are a resident selling your main home, 50% of any capital gains realised will be treated as income for tax purposes, which means they will be taxed on the income tax sliding scale, with a fifth of the tax coming due in each of the five years following the sale. Unless, that is,

you reinvest the profit in another home within two years – in which case you will be exempt. As a non-resident your gain will be taxed as income, at a flat rate of 25%.

Inheritance tax (*imposto sobre as sucessoes e doacoes*) is levied at different rates depending upon the value of the property and on the relationship between the parties, from 0% for inheritances of less than 70,000 euros by spouses or minor children up to 50% on very large inheritances by people who are not related.

It is up to you to file a tax return; seek professional advice. If your Portuguese is up to it, speak to your local tax office (*reparticao de financas*). The website of the national tax office publishes information on the tax system in English, but this cannot always be relied upon to be up to date. Visit www.dgci.min-financas.pt. and follow the links to *Organica*, then *Organica English*. British citizens ordinarily resident in

Health and social security

Portugal are entitled to state medical treatment on the same terms as the locals, but in order to benefit from this you will need to apply for a national insurance card (*cartao de utente*) at your local health centre (*centro de saude*).

In order to apply for the card, you must already have a Portuguese residence permit, and until you have a national insurance card, you will only be eligible for free emergency treatment. The exception to this is if you receive UK state pension, in which case you can apply for the card on arrival.

To sign up for social security contributions, you must get in touch with the Regional Centre of Social Security (*Centro Regional de Segurança Social*); if you are an employee, around 10% of your salary will be deducted to cover national health insurance. Further information can be obtained from the special department for foreign citizens (*Departamento de Relações Internacionais e Convenções da Segurança Social*), tel 00 351 21 362 16 33.

Under the Portuguese health system, which is run by the *Ministerio de Saude*, hospital treatment is free, although you must pay to use a *centro de saude*; the costs of treatments are reimbursed at different levels ranging from 50–100%. Many people use pharmacists for basic, free health advice.

In Portugal, as in any other foreign country, think carefully about what the state system entitles you to, and consider taking out private health cover – especially if you are resident there but not working. If you have a second home in Portugal, ensure you have a European Health Insurance Card and take out a comprehensive travel insurance policy to cover you and your family whenever you visit.

To find websites of any government offices in Portugal, follow the links from the government's main site at http://www.portugal.gov.pt/Portal/EN/Directorio/.

Other public services

- Your social security rights in Portugal are the same as those that apply elsewhere within the EEA. When you start work in Portugal, you will contribute to the Portuguese social security system and consequently, gain the right to benefits. If you are a pensioner you can have your UK state pension paid in Portugal. There is a special information department for foreign nationals: the *Departamento de Relações Internacionais e Convenções da Segurança Social*, tel: 00 351 21 362 1633.
- You may wish to send your child to a Portuguese school or you may prefer an international school. For information about the state sector, contact the Ministry of Education in Lisbon, or talk to the Portuguese Consulate in London. Alternatively, visit the European Commission PLOTEUS portal: www.europa.eu.int/ploteus. The British Embassy lists international schools in Portugal on its website.
- You can contact the Portuguese National Academic Recognition Information Centre on tel: 00 351 21 312 60 00 or visit www.dges.mcies.pt.

Finding professionals

- The British Embassy in Portugal can help you find English-speaking lawyers, translators, doctors, dentists and private hospitals; as well as providing a range of other advice and services. Contact details are listed on the website, which is accessible via www.britishembassy. gov.uk.
- To find a qualified estate agent, look for a firm which is a member of the *Associação dos Profissionais e Empresas de Mediação Imobiliária de Portugal*. The organisation's website, www.apemip.pt, has a searchable members' directory.
- To find a surveyor, search the Royal Institution of Chartered Surveyors' directory via www.ricsfirms.co.uk.
- Possible sources of architects include the Royal Institute of British Architects (www.riba.org) and the *Ordem dos Arquitectos* (www.oasrs.org).
- If you want someone to handle red tape on your behalf, look out for an *assistenca burocratica*, which is similar to a Spanish *gestor*.
- Portuguese Yellow Pages can be electronically accessed at www.paginasa marelas.pt and is available in English.

Utilities

- Most households use bottled gas. Gas installers are licensed by the Directorate of Energy (*Direcção-Geral de Energia*), who also appoint independent gas inspectors. You will need an inspection every five years and more frequently if you are letting to tourists. Ask your lawyer or estate agent for advice on this.
- Electricity comes from *Electricidade de Portugal* (EDP), which normally provides connections to premises within 1km of one of their transformers, and can provide quotations for the installation of an additional transformer and a special line. You can request a new domestic supply by phone (+ 800 246 246) or at the local office of your electricity distribution company. You will need an armful of documentation, and must decide what tariff you want to be on.
- Water supply is the responsibility of your local council (*camara*); you will need proof of identity and ownership and your tax number to register for a new supply.

Miscellaneous information

- The British-Portuguese Chamber of Commerce sponsors a useful guide to living in Portugal, which contains contact details of member companies. To access the guide visit www.livinginfoguides.com.
- If you are considering setting up in business, contact *Investimento, Comercio e Turismo* via www.icep.pt. The organisation also runs a portal providing consumer information on everything from tourism to business start-ups, and a host of travel information: www.portugal.org.
- The Association of Foreign Property Owners in Portugal is a non-profit making organisation designed to help you overcome any difficulties you encounter. For details visit www.afpop.com.
- The official tourist board site is at www.visitportugal.pt.

Florida, USA

An American favourite, the 'Sunshine State' is ever-popular with families and people retiring for the winter.

The property market

As an almost year-round holiday destination, Florida's most popular regions for property buyers include the central area containing Orlando, Disney World and Universal Studios; the south-east, stretching from Palm Beach to the Florida Keys, taking in Miami, Key West and the Everglades National Park; and the south-western coast including gulf resorts like Naples and Venice. Some of the western coasts are relatively unspoilt, and prices throughout the region are, square metre for square metre, affordable for many UK buyers. For other locations in the USA see page 215.

The buying process

Anyone who deals in real estate in Florida must be licensed – apart from people employed by a single developer or builder. They should have indemnity insurance and conform to the Florida Real Estate Commission's code of practice. As well as estate agents as we would understand them, Florida has 'buyers brokers' who act solely for the buyer. Agents can act on a single, dual or transactional basis.

It is common practice to put down a small deposit of a few thousand dollars as a goodwill gesture, before proceeding to a full purchase contract. Conveyancing tends to be done by a 'title insurance company' rather than a lawyer – these firms check the public records to make sure the seller owns the property and will then insure it against anyone else making a third party claim. Proving title may take two or three months.

The sales contract will be similar to those on mainland Europe, including a series of carefully worded contingency clauses. When the contract is agreed you lodge a 10% deposit with an 'escrow' agent, who then compiles and checks the necessary documentation to make sure the transaction can 'close' within the specified period. The escrow agent performs the same duties as a European notary, paying taxes and the like at the final signing.

Do a final inventory check on the property as close as possible to the time of closing, because property is sold subject to the condition you accept it in at that point.

Fees and taxes

- For legal/title insurance fees, transfer fees and property taxes, allow around 2% of purchase price; if you are buying with a mortgage, add a further 3% to cover administrative costs. Estate agents' commission 6%, paid by the seller.

- Sales tax (the US version of VAT) is levied at 6% in Florida, but some counties add a surtax of up to 1.5% on top.
- All property owners in Florida must pay ongoing property taxes, which fall into two categories – 'ad valorem' taxes based on the value of the property, and non-ad valorem taxes. Taxes may be set at county, city or district level and cover everything from education and fire services to water supplies. These tend to add up to around 1 to 3% of the property's value per year.

Red tape

Assuming you remain a 'non-resident alien' for US tax purposes, your income may be dealt with in one of two ways – either as income that is 'effectively connected' with a trade or business in the US, or as income that is 'not effectively connected' with a trade or business in the United States. If you choose to declare rental income as the former, it will be taxed at the same graduated rates (with allowable deductions for expenses) as US residents would pay. If you opt for the latter, your income will be taxed at a flat 30% and no deductions will be allowed.

Tangible property tax is charged on business assets, for which a holiday home that is rented out may qualify; you will need to keep receipts for capital expenditure on the property. You may also need to pay tourist taxes and sales tax on your rentals.

Capital gains tax for non-residents is charged at 30%, although you can offset repair and improvement costs against the gain. There is a 10% withholding tax when properties are sold.

As a non-resident, you must pay inheritance tax ('estate tax' in the US) on the value of property located in the US at the time of your death. Transfers between spouses are exempt from tax. The highest rate of estate tax was 49% for 2003, reducing gradually to 45% in the year 2009. As when buying a property in Europe, it is vital to take advice on inheritance issues in advance; it is crucial to put the property in the right names (single owner, joint owners, joint owners with children, children's names only, etc) from the start. You also need to make two wills – one for your UK assets and one for those in the US.

For more information on your federal tax liabilities in the US, visit www.irs.gov/businesses/small/international/index.html. For information about all aspects of life in Florida, visit the state's official website, www.myflorida.com.

For useful articles about the Floridian economy, visit www.floridataxwatch.org.

Immigration

Whereas within the EU we have the right to live wherever we want and have the state treat us like natives, the immigration rules mean it can be extremely difficult to become a resident of the US.

There are circumstances in which it is achievable:

- If any members of your immediate family are US residents or citizens you may be entitled to residency; although it can take anything from a year to ten or more to get through the waiting list! If you are marrying a US citizen or are the minor child of one, you will achieve residency quickest.

- If you travel to the US with a 'B' visa, you can stay up to six months at a time, although you cannot simply stay there six months, go home for a week then come back!
- If you enrol on an academic programme, you could enter the US on a student visa, which allows you to stay for the duration of the programme; you will have to show you have sufficient funds to pay for tuition and living expenses without working, though.
- You can get a visa of indefinite duration for the purpose of setting up a business in the US. This is called an 'E' visa. It is possible to have your US real estate investments considered an enterprise, although you will generally need to own more than one property, or be in the process of buying more than one, to qualify. You will need an experienced US immigration lawyer to get you in this way, and it is best if you explore all this before actually making a purchase so that you can, if necessary, change the way you are buying it.
- Non-US businesses can transfer executive personnel to the US to operate the US branch, affiliate or subsidiary operation; this provision is meant for multinational companies but works for small businesses too; there are limits on how this 'L' visa can work, however.
- An 'H' visa is a long term visa for professional workers (normally people with degrees or equivalent experience) who have a particular skill that an employer needs and is prepared to pay you a salary for, that is the same as, or higher than, that paid to US citizens in the same area. If the employer is a start-up company, you can get away without providing financial details, but by the end of three years you need to show that the company has enough income to pay your salary.
- If you have an L or E visa, your spouse will be entitled to work in the US in any job.

Applying for any of these visas, except the tourist and student ones, can be expensive and it is advisable to employ a specialist immigration lawyer to make the application on your behalf, because otherwise you may miss out on important details pertinent to the process and end up having your application denied. Legal help may cost several thousands of pounds, however – so you need to be serious and fairly confident about your application before you start.

For more information, visit www.usembassy.org.uk.

Health and social security

There is no reciprocal health agreement between the UK and USA, so if you are visiting, living or working in Florida, as a priority one of the first things you must sort out is some form of health insurance. If you need to use the US health system and are under-insured, the medical bills you could face could be astronomical.

Anyone staying for up to six months should have a comprehensive travel policy or an international health policy to cover you at home and in other countries, including the US. Most international policies cover you for repatriation should it be necessary, and for your body to be shipped back home if the worst happened and you died over there.

Check the details of the policy carefully, though; look at what excesses are in place, make sure the annual limit on medical costs is as high as you can afford, and check whether the insurer will settle the bills direct with the health provider in the US, or reimburse you.

Most US residents have health insurance paid for partly or wholly by their employers, but there are estimated to be more than a million Americans with no or inadequate health insurance. People aged 65 and over, and people of any age with disabilities, are covered by Medicare, the publicly-funded health scheme.

If you are planning to move to the US and do not fit into any of these categories, check out the cost of healthcare in advance – it may be so expensive that it puts you off the whole venture.

As a resident, depending on how long you have lived in the US and whether you have a US employer, you may need to contribute to the US social security system. Department of Work and Pensions leaflet SA33, available via www.dwp.gov.uk/ lifeevent/benefits/social_security_ agreements.asp, gives more details.

Other information

For information about all aspects of life in Florida, visit the state's official website, www.myflorida.com. The site includes details of licensed professionals ranging from architects to yacht brokers; contains information about tourist attractions; offers advice on moving to Florida (including comprehensive listings and advice about real estate agents, developers and self-build in the state); and includes travel information, for example details about airlines and car rental companies.

- Florida Tourist Board is at www.flausa.com.
- Expat websites include the British Club of Orlando (www.OrlandoBritish Club.com), Union Jack magazine (www.ujnews.com), the British Bureau (www.britishbureau.com), Sunny Brits (www.sunnybrits.com) and British in Florida (www.britishflorida.com).

The Mediterranean

Europe's holiday playground, offering a wide range of activities and cultural experiences for all ages.

Over the last twenty years the Mediterranean has been the main destination for Europeans, especially the British, seeking sunny summer holidays. Looking at the climate of the coastal fringes of the sea it is not hard to see why – long hot summers, with more or less guaranteed sunshine, and mild, wetter winters.

In fact this mildness has encouraged not just tourists but people retiring there permanently, away from the cool and occasionally cold winters of Britain.

While the Spanish Costas, Balearic Islands and the Algarve have been popular locations for British property hunters for many years now, more recently a host of other countries dotted around the Mediterranean have entered the fray.

The island nations of Cyprus and Malta, both of which joined the European Union in 2004, are popular choices for second home owners and especially among British and other north European retirees; properties there have clocked up impressive capital growth in recent years as a result.

Mainland Greece and some of its more popular islands have quietly slipped onto the overseas property ladder after two decades as a top holiday destination. Turkey, a relative newcomer, has if anything made a bigger splash, with low prices, increasing accessibility and the ever-present hope of EU entry marking it out as having huge investment potential over the medium to long term.

Cyprus

The property market

Cyprus' balmy climate and long-standing status as a popular tourist destination, combined with its entry into the European Union and the pegging of its economy to the euro, have earned it a firm place on Britons' list of favourite overseas property locations. The distinct British influence on the island (English is widely spoken and you even drive on the left) along with low taxes for pensioners have helped make it especially popular among retirees. Developments have sprung up all over the island, which is the third biggest in the Mediterranean, with tourism centring mainly on Larnaka, Limassol, Nicosia and Pafos. More recently agents have been selling properties in Turkish-occupied Northern Cyprus (see below).

How to buy

The legal system in Cyprus is based on English law. If you are buying from a developer you will typically be expected to pay a small reservation deposit (non-returnable), followed by 20–30% of the purchase price on signing of the preliminary contract and the remainder as negotiated and set out in the contract.

Have your lawyer check all legal documents from developers extremely carefully – there have been reports of contracts that seek to prevent owners from reselling their properties without permission and the payment of a large fee to the developer.

For resales expect to pay a 10% deposit when you sign the initial contract and the rest on completion, as would happen in the UK.

Buying in Northern Cyprus

Some property investors, mainly British, have been tempted to buy properties in the north of Cyprus, where prices are considerably lower than in the south. This is an extremely risky venture, unless you have a cast iron guarantee to the title – which is practically impossible unless the person selling it to you can prove they have owned the property since before 1974. The Turkish Republic of Northern Cyprus is legally recognised by very few countries except Turkey, and therefore the legal position of title deeds issued there over the last three decades is extremely precarious.

Since border restrictions were lifted and Greek Cypriots have been allowed to cross the demarcation line, many have visited land or homes lost after the Turkish invasion, and are pressing for restitution or compensation in any negotiated settlement that may result from Turkey's attempts to gain entry into the EU.

As a non-resident you must apply to the Council of Ministers for permission to buy, which can take up to a year and requires bank and character references – this is essentially a formality and the sale will go through on the basis that permission will be forthcoming, but ensure your lawyer includes a clause in the contract to cover you in case it was not granted.

The Cypriot government runs checks against criminal records, makes sure that land size is within the required limits, that purchasers only own one home in Cyprus and that they have enough money to live on. Even if approval were not granted you would be able to appeal, and in any case would have 17 years in which to sell the property.

Fees and taxes

- **Estate agents' fees** – Most British buyers purchase through an agent or developer, or a partnership of both. Sellers pay agents' commissions, which can be 5% or more.
- **VAT** – around 10% on new-build properties
- **Real estate transfer fee** – payable to the land registry, on a sliding scale from 3% to 8% according to the property value
- **Immovable property tax** – an annual tax based on the value of the property from a 1980 baseline, at rates from 0.2% to 0.35% (although an initial sum is exempt).
- **Stamp duty** – 2% (after an initial exempt sum)
- **Mortgage registration fee** – 1%
- Local authority taxes (equivalent to council tax) range from 0.1% to 0.5% per annum, to cover refuse collection, sewerage, street lighting etc. Remember you may also have to pay service charges on a villa or apartment complex.

Red tape

Residence permits are available from the Civil Registry and Migration Department of the Ministry of Interior, and at main police stations. Application forms are available at www.moi.gov.cy and must be submitted within three months of entry into Cyprus.

Income tax is charged on a progressive scale up to 30%, although there are exemption allowances and you can deduct a notional 20% of the rental income as expenses. In Cyprus retirees are taxed at only 5% per annum on all imported pensions, and the country only taxes assets that are brought into Cyprus, rather than your worldwide income.

Capital gains tax is charged at a rate of 20%, although you will be exempt if you are a Cypriot resident at the time of sale – even if you were non-resident when you bought. Inheritance tax is no longer charged.

Health and social security

If you are employed and pay social insurance contributions in Cyprus – or if you are a pensioner retiring there – you must apply for a Cyprus Medical Card via the Ministry of Health, whose website is www.moh.gov.cy. You will need supporting documents, for example proving that your pension is being paid to you in Cyprus.

In Cyprus patients pay towards the cost of appointments and hospital stays, for example £10 for a visit to a specialist and £7 for a visit to a GP. In addition they pay the fees specified for laboratory, radiology and all examinations and tests. Inpatient fees for paying patients are £60, £50 and £35 for accommodation and nursing in first, second and third class wards respectively; intensive care costs £100 a day. Depending on your age, income and medical condition, you may be entitled to free or half-price care.

Other public services

- For European-wide information on education, social security and tax regimes, searchable by country, visit: www.eurydice.org. There are several international schools on the island, at grammar and undergraduate level.
- To find out about equivalence of qualifications in Cyprus, follow the links on the Europe Open for Professions website at www.dfes.gov.uk; alternatively contact the European Network of national information centres on academic recognition and qualifications, via www.enic-naric.net.
- The Cypriot government's official website is at www.cyprus.gov.cy.

Utilities

- Electricity Authority of Cyprus: www.eac.com.cy
- Cyprus Telecommunications: www.cyta.com.cy
- There is no piped gas in Cyprus
- There is no TV licence fee – the public broadcasting service is financed with a tax included in your electricity bill from the Electricity Authority of Cyprus.

Finding professionals

- The British Embassy lists contact details for English-speaking lawyers in Cyprus, available via www.britishembassy.gov.uk.
- The FIABCI-registered Cyprus Real Estate Agents Association is on tel +35 722 889 759. The Cyprus Land & Building Developers Association is on tel +35 722 665 102.
- The Cyprus Architects Association is contactable via www.architecture.org.cy.
- Cyprus Chamber of Commerce and Industry: www.ccci.org.cy

Other resources

- For useful information on all aspects of moving to and living in Cyprus, contact the UK-Cyprus Citizens Association via www.ukca.com.cy.
- The Cyprus Tourist Authority website is at www.visitcyprus.org.cy.
- Cyprus Airways: www.cyprusairways.com, tel +35 722 365 700.

185

Turkey

The property market

Likened to Spain in the 1970s by virtue of the huge growth potential of its tourist industry, Turkey has been flying up the overseas property hitlist in recent years. Popular locations include Altinkum, which features three sandy beaches; the pretty South Aegean seaside resort of Bodrum; thriving fishing town Fethiye; and popular tourist resort Marmaris. More adventurous investors have bought in the former imperial capital, Istanbul. With prices already spiralling upwards, predictions of EU entry and eventually even a conversion to the euro add fuel to a market already appealing to second home owners, investors and retirees alike.

 ## Risk assessment

The British Embassy in Turkey warns of the threat from terrorism in Turkey, with both international and local terrorist groups active in the country. There have been bomb attacks in Istanbul and other tourist areas. For further details see the Foreign & Commonwealth Office website (www.fco.gov.uk).

Potential investors should note that the frequency of major earthquakes adds considerable risk to property ownership in Istanbul and surrounding areas.

How to buy

Under Turkish law you can, as a foreigner, own up to a maximum of 2.5 hectares of land and property in Turkey, although the Council of Ministers may increase this threshold to a maximum of 30 hectares.

The main difference between buying in Turkey and in other parts of Europe is the requirement to obtain permission from the military to purchase the property. Huge areas of rural Turkey are designated as military land, which non-nationals are not permitted to buy.

There are also restrictions on foreigners' ability to buy in some less developed (but non-military) areas; in most areas British buyers are interested in there is no problem.

You will usually need to pay a 10% deposit on signing the preliminary contract, and then your lawyer must secure clean title to the property, and make sure it is debt-free. Under-declaration of price on completion – which reduces sellers' tax liabilities – is common, but unadvisable as it could leave you with an undervalued property and increased capital gains tax liability when you come to sell.

For more information visit the Turkish Embassy at: www.turkisheconomy. org.uk.

Taxes and fees

- **Estate agents' fee** – allow 6%, and assume this will be split 50/50 between buyer and seller
- **Property transfer tax** – 3% of declared value of property, which may be shared between buyer and seller
- **VAT** is not charged
- **Legal fees** – allow 4–5% of the purchase price to cover legal and notary fees, insurances and registration charges
- **Annual property tax** – 0.5% of declared price.

Red tape

Unlike when travelling to EU countries, you will need a tourist visa to enter Turkey. You can obtain a three month visa at the port of entry in Turkey.

If you want to stay for more than three months, you will need a residence visa, obtainable from the Turkish consulate; contact them well in advance to establish how quickly this will be available. You must register with the local police within a month of arriving in Turkey, in order to obtain a residence permit.

You can take household items into Turkey provided you have a residence permit valid for no less than a year.

To work in Turkey you will need a work permit, issued by the Ministry of the Interior in Ankara. You should contact the Turkish Embassy in London and/or your prospective employer in Turkey about application procedures. The government's social security department has a website at www.csgb.gov.tr.

Even as a non-resident you will be liable to income tax on any rental income your property earns (minus legitimate expenses); tax will be charged at a rate ranging from 15 to 35%.

Capital gains tax is levied at 25% of the profit between the purchase and sales price, if you sell within a year. After that you are exempt, unless you have bought the property as a company.

Your heirs will have to pay inheritance tax at a rate ranging from 1 to 30%, depending on their relationship to you, and the value of the property.

Health and social security

Turkey has no reciprocal healthcare agreement with the UK, so do not travel without comprehensive medical insurance (including cover for medical repatriation), as private medical treatment is very expensive. The British Embassy website has details of English speaking hospitals and doctors, at www.britishembassy.org.tr. If you visit rural areas you should ensure that inoculations are up to date. For information about the Turkish social security system, talk to embassy or consulate staff, or visit www.csgb.gov.tr.

Other information

- For a list of Turkish estate agents with FIABCI membership, visit www.fiabciturkey.com; the site also lists members of the Central European Real Estate Associations Network (for more information on CEREAN, visit www.cerean.com). The FIABCI-registered Istanbul Chamber of General Real Estate Commission Agents is contactable on tel: +90 212 3270061 or via www.emlakpusulasi.org.
- The British Embassy lists contact details for English-speaking lawyers in Turkey, available via www.britishembassy.org.tr.
- For tourism information, visit http://www.gototurkey.co.uk/

Greece

The property market

A relatively slow starter in the overseas property game, Greece's most popular location for British buyers – especially those wishing to retire – is Crete. Other islands popular with tourists, including Rhodes, Kos, Mykonos, Corfu, Zante and Skiathos, attract buyers and there has been considerable growth in interest in mainland Greece – especially the Peloponnese. Coastal properties attract premium prices but there are plenty of bargains to be had inland.

How to buy

You will need your lawyer to run searches, check title carefully (there can be problems ensuring that everyone who has a say over the sale is in agreement, as there has been a tradition of dispersal among Greek families) and ensure there are no outstanding debts, rights-of-way issues or other legal encumbrances.

You need a tax number (AFM), which is issued on the spot at tax offices, free of charge. As a formality you may also need a temporary residence permit (the Blue Card) from the local police station, to buy property near national borders and on some islands such as Crete and Rhodes.

You must pay a 10% deposit on signing of the pre-contract. The final sales transfer is conducted by a notary. Under-declaration of property values for tax purposes is common, but not advised.

Buying costs

- **Transfer tax**: 9–11% (or 7–9% if the area is not covered by the fire brigade)
- **Legal fees**: allow 2%
- **Notary fees**: 1%
- **Mortgage registration**: 0.5%
- **Municipality tax**: 3% of the transfer tax

Ongoing costs

- **Annual municipal tax**: 0.025%–0.035% of the declared value of the property (incorporated into electricity bills).
- **Annual property tax**: 0.3% to 0.8% of the declared value of the property (if above a set amount)
- You are liable to income tax on rental income; capital gains tax is charged at 20% for the first five years, falling to 10% for the period from 5–15 years and 5% for the period from 15–25 years. Inheritance tax is charged at 0–40% depending on the recipient's relationship to the deceased, and the amount inherited.

Other information

- The Greek National Health system provides a basic medical service to Greek NI contributors, and as a visitor your European health insurance card will cover you. Private medical insurance is recommended for people planning to emigrate, as standards vary considerably; on some islands even private facilities are limited and ambulance shortages are common.
- The British Embassy in Athens lists English-speaking lawyers and schools in Greece. Its website is accessible via: www.british embassy.gov.uk.
- To find a reputable estate agent, the Greek branch of FIABCI is accessible via www.fiabci.gr; the Hellenic Federation of Real Estate Agents, itself a member of FIABCI, is contactable on tel: +30 21 03621930 or via www.omase.gr.
- The Greek National Tourism Organisation website is at www.gnto.gr.

Malta

The property market

The Republic of Malta, which became a member of the EU in 2004, consists of the islands of Malta, Gozo and Comino, along with two small, uninhabited islands. More than a million tourists visit Malta each year, almost half of them British. Holiday houses and apartments, along with traditional farmhouses, are popular buys; there are also several high-profile purpose-built resort developments. Sought-after locations include the capital, Valletta; Sliema; St Julian's Bay and St Paul's Bay, as well as any number of Maltese and Gozitan villages.

How to buy

The usual preliminary contract commits both parties, with a 10% deposit paid at this point, returnable only in circumstances outlined in the contract. If you are buying a holiday home, you must apply to the Ministry of Finance for a permit. In these cases, the property has to be valued above certain fixed levels (so as to minimise the impact of foreign ownership on locals'

ability to afford homes). You may only sell your property to another non-resident if you have already made an effort to sell to local buyers.

The Maltese government restricts foreigners' ability to buy second homes by imposing a minimum price limit (around £50,000 for apartments and £90,000 for houses at the time of writing).

Buying costs

- Stamp duty: 5%
- Notary fees: 1%
- Searches and other fees (eg for buying permit): a few hundred pounds

Ongoing costs

Income tax is charged only if residency is taken up, in which case there is a favourable rate of tax of just 15% (provided your Maltese income is above a certain level). As a resident you may rent your property out provided it is licensed as holiday accommodation by the Malta Tourism Authority. The 15% tax rate on

profits minus allowable expenses applies.

There is no inheritance tax in Malta, but there is a 5% transfer tax on the value of the property, as at time of death. If it is jointly owned and one of the spouses passes away, the 5% is levied on half the value of the property.

Other information

- Healthcare in Malta is free at the point of delivery to Maltese citizens, and to EU citizens who visit or take up residence and make social security contributions there. To register as a resident contact the Entitlements' Unit within the Ministry of Health, via tel: +356 21 22 40 71 or email: entitlements.mhec@gov.mt.
- For further information on all aspects

of life in Malta, visit the Maltese government's website: www.gov.mt. The official Maltese tourism site is at www.visitmalta.com.
- The British High Commission in Valletta keeps a list of English-speaking lawyers: follow the link from www.britishembassy.gov.uk.
- You can contact the Maltese Association of Estate Agents on tel +356 343730.

The Balkans

Natural beauty, historic towns and coastal resorts, plus rapid economic growth.

For centuries the Balkan region – which stretches from Slovenia and Croatia in the west to Bulgaria and Romania in the east – has been fought over, and held back by nationalism and communism.

The federation of six republics that constituted post-1945 Yugoslavia broke down in 1992, with fierce wars in Croatia, Bosnia-Herzegovina and Kosovo concluding with an uneasy peace in the early years of the 21st century. Meanwhile the former communist republics of Bulgaria and Romania began to rebuild their economies and head towards European Union

membership – potentially to be joined by Croatia and an independent Montenegro.

Beautiful and varied countryside and coastal regions – the Adriatic to the west and the Black Sea to the east – give the whole region huge tourism potential, and from an investment perspective the long process of economic and legal modernisation involved in EU integration creates the possibility of prolonged growth in property prices.

Of all the Balkan nations, Bulgaria has done most to expand its appeal to western tourists, launching itself as a summer package tour destination. Its Black Sea

coast has proved extremely popular with Irish and British 'off-plan' investors.

Croatia and Slovenia market themselves to more upmarket buyers, trading off their stunning natural beauty. Montenegro and Romania, meanwhile, offer buyers the chance to sample lesser known nations with impressive long-term investment potential.

Bulgaria

The property market

Bulgaria has captured the imagination of British bargain hunters in recent years. With housing stock ranging from seaside apartments and villas on the Black Sea coast, to ski lodges in resorts like Bansko and Borovets, traditional village homes inland, and flats in the capital, Sofia, the country offers property to suit all tastes, at prices way lower than in most of the rest of Europe. Off-plan developments in the Black Sea regions have proved particularly popular with investors hoping to capitalise on Bulgaria's entry into the EU, although some pundits forecast an eventual over-supply of property, and point to poor quality construction and lax planning controls.

How to buy

According to the Bulgarian Constitution, foreigners can buy buildings but not land – although this should change as the economy falls more closely into line with western Europe. One option is to set up a Bulgarian company and buy the property and land through that; but appoint your own lawyer and make sure he or she conducts full searches to establish that the person 'selling' you the property is the rightful owner. Your lawyer should make sure any company you set up is properly administered, and that suitable arrangements are in place for it to discharge its ongoing responsibilities.

More care is needed if you buy off-plan – make sure your lawyer negotiates suitable arrangements for stage payments and safeguards to protect you if the developer goes bust. Expect to pay 10–40% deposit when you sign the preliminary contract.

At completion, under-declaration of property prices is common, but you should insist the real price is declared, partly to safeguard against future capital gains tax liability, and partly to ensure the estate agent has not artificially inflated the price.

Buying costs

- **Estate agents' fees** – vary from 3–10%; typically around 6% in total, of which half is paid by the seller and half by the buyer
- **Land tax and notary fees** – 5%
- **VAT** – generally not charged, but may be levied at 20%
- **Municipal property tax** – 2%

Ongoing costs

If you rent the property out, income tax is payable at 15%; as is capital gains tax (also 15%) if you come to sell. There is an annual property tax at 0.15% of the declared value; you must also pay a separate rubbish tax. There is no inheritance tax in Bulgaria.

Other information

- The British Embassy in Sofia has a list of English-speaking lawyers in Bulgaria, accessible via www.british-embassy.bg.
- The National Real Property Association of Bulgaria, which doubles as the Bulgarian chapter of FIABCI, is contactable via www.nsni.bg.
- The Bulgarian Union of Architects has a website at www.bulgarianarchitects.org
- For information about health and other public services in Bulgaria, follow the links from the English version of the government website, at www.government.bg.
- The Bulgarian tourist board website is at www.bulgariatravel.org.

Croatia

The property market

Although Croatia is often bracketed together with Bulgaria, the market is rather different. A breathtakingly beautiful country with a huge coastline and more than 1,000 islands, Croatia has bargains aplenty but prices in prime, upmarket locations like Dubrovnik and parts of Istria are closer to western levels – albeit still in many cases excellent value for money. The Croatian government has also imposed tight controls on development, so there are fewer properties available, although the 'EU effect' could still apply.

How to buy

One vital issue makes Croatian property purchase a complex affair – all foreign purchasers must obtain permission to buy from the Ministry of Foreign Affairs. This process can take between six months and a year, and only once approval has been granted can the purchase be finalised and your title be registered in the official Croatian Land Book. You may go through the rest of the purchase and wait for approval before completing the sale; an alternative is to buy through a company, which gets round the need for MFA approval.

Establishing clear title to property can also prove problematic – war-related ownership disputes and highly dispersed families mean there is a danger of the vendor not having the undisputed right to sell you the property, so it is vital to have your lawyer check title before committing to buy.

Some foreign buyers have been ripped off by fly-by-night estate agents operating in the relatively unregulated Croatian property market, so make sure any agency you deal with is a registered company, and only ever lodge deposit money with your lawyer.

Buying costs

- **Estate agents' fees**: 2–3% each from buyer and seller
- **Property purchase tax**: 5%
- **Legal fees**: 1–2%
- **VAT (PDV)**: 22% – payable only if the seller is PDV-registered

Ongoing costs

On the sale of a property within three years of purchase, Capital Gains Tax (CGT) at a rate of 35% is levied on the profit between the purchase and sale price. After three or more years of ownership, no CGT is payable.

Income tax at a rate of 25% is payable on the declared profit of any rental income received. Pensions received from abroad are exempt from tax.

Other information

- If you want to live permanently in Croatia you will need to apply for a temporary residence permit (which covers you for up to a year); after five years of temporary residence you qualify for permanent residency.
- For details on health and other public services, visit the Croatian government's website at www.vlada.hr.
- The British Embassy in Zagreb keeps a list of English-speaking lawyers; visit www.britishembassy. gov.uk.
- The Croatian Chamber of Architects and Civil Engineers has a website at www.arhitekti-hkaig.com
- The Croatian Chamber of Economy produces useful guides, which are available at www.hgk.hr/en/pocetna.asp.

Montenegro

The property market

Although closely connected to its more troubled neighbour Serbia, the tiny country of Montenegro has huge potential as an overseas property hotspot in its own right. Formerly a playground for the rich and famous, the country escaped the worst ravages of the 1990s Balkan conflict, but is still on a long path to recovery. EU entry – with or without Serbia – is a distinct possibility, and the euro is already legal tender. Prices along the 293km Adriatic coastline are extremely affordable in comparison to Croatia or other southern Mediterranean countries; inland properties situated amid mountains and forests cost even less. The country remains relatively inaccessible other than via Dubrovnik airport, around 20km north of the border; although there is a daily service from London to Belgrade (the Serbian capital) and connecting flights to Tivat or Podgorica (the Montenegrin capital). There are direct flights to Tivat during the summer season.

How to buy

The buying and selling of properties is without restriction in Montenegro and is legally secure; the government is keen to attract foreign investment. The only exception to this is when buying undeveloped land. Some buyers have got round this by first negotiating a separate contract with the seller to have foundations laid, which is enough to make the land qualify as developed.

As in any other country, you must establish clear legal title, make sure what you are buying is what is recorded in the local land registry, and have your lawyer conduct all other necessary checks. You will need to negotiate a contract and pay a 10% deposit, before going on to conduct the full set of checks, complete the sale and register your ownership at the land registry.

Buying costs

- **Estate agents' fees**: expect to pay 5%, but ask for details upfront as some companies include the commission in the initial purchase price, which makes the costs opaque

- **Purchase tax**: 5% of the valuation given by the Inland Revenue office when the property is sold. VAT of 17% is payable on new build apartments, although in such cases the purchase tax is refunded.

Ongoing costs

Income tax on Montenegrin income is charged at progressive rates from 16–24%. You must also pay an annual property tax to your local authority. The level of this will depend on value and location, but will be less than 1%.

Other information

- If you want to live in Montenegro, you must apply for a residence permit from the Belgrade Police Department. There are preferential tax rates for foreign residents.

- Contact the British Embassy in Montenegro for a list of local lawyers, via www.britishembassy.gov.uk.
- The Montenegrin government website is at www.vlada.cg.yu/eng; the

195

Montenegro Agency for Economic Restructuring and Foreign Investments is at www.agencijacg.org/englishver/homepage.htm. For general information on Montenegro visit www.montenegro.yu. The official tourist board website is at www.visit-montenegro.com

Slovenia

The property market

The tiny country of Slovenia is often referred to as the Balkan Switzerland on account of its stunning lakes and mountains; but it also has a small stretch of Adriatic coastline just south of the Italian city of Trieste. Accessible via Italy, Graz airport in neighbouring Austria, or its own capital, Ljubljana, the country offers property hunters everything from city apartments to ski chalets, country cottages and seaside villas. Now a member of the EU, Slovenia is becoming a prosperous nation, with house prices already approaching those of its westerly neighbours. But there are still bargains to be had, particularly inland and off the beaten track.

How to buy

Since joining the EU, it has become fairly straightforward for foreign buyers to purchase property in Slovenia. Estate agents usually administer land registry and title deeds checks, but you will still need a lawyer to ensure that these are carried out, and to draw up a purchase contract, at which point you must pay a 10% deposit.

You are required by the Ministry of Justice and Foreign Affairs to register at the local government offices, where you will be issued with a permit giving you 'ownership status'. The official contract signing takes place at the local notary office, and an official court translator must be present at the signing should also be requested.

Buying costs

- **Estate agents' fees**: 4% (2% each from buyer and seller)
- **VAT on new build properties**: 8.5%
- **Notary/official translator fees**: a few hundred pounds
- **Legal fees**: allow 1–2%
- **Stamp duty**: 2% of sales price

Ongoing costs

Income tax is charged progressively at rates from 17 to 50%. Capital gains tax is charged at 25%. Inheritance tax is imposed using a progressive scale from 5–30% depending on the inheritor's relationship with the deceased.

Other information

- The Slovenian estate agents' association (*Slovensko Nepremicninsko Zdruzenje*) can be contacted on tel +386 41 677846 or via www.skb-nepr.si. The Slovenian chapter of FIABCI is at www.drustvo-fiabci.si.

- To find a Slovenian architect, contact the Chamber of Architecture and Spatial Planning via www.archiforum.com.

- If you want to live in Slovenia your first contact should be the *Urad Za Tujce* (office for foreigners), tel + 01/306 30 45. To obtain a tax number, you should go to *Davcna uprava Bezigrad* in Ljubljana, tel + 01/306 28 50 if you already have the temporary permit in Slovenia; or *Davcna uprava*, Dunajska street 22, Ljubljana, tel + 01/47 44 728 if you do not.

- The Slovenian state portal is at http://e-uprava.gov.si/e-uprava/en/portal.euprava. The Slovenian Ministry of Finance's website is at www.sigov.si.

- The British Embassy in Ljubljana lists estate agencies, lawyers and doctors and international schools in Slovenia. It also lists the following resources for British expatriates: informal get-togethers of English-speaking expatriates on occasional Fridays; e-mail expats@wagner-media.com for more details. The Slovene International Ladies Association can be contacted on: + 511-0039. The Slovenia Times is a Slovenian newspaper in English language, website at www.sloveniatimes.com.

Romania

The property market

Prices in Romania have risen enormously in anticipation of Romania's accession to the EU, but property throughout the country is still reputed to be amongst the most under-valued in Europe. Popular areas for overseas buyers include the elegant capital, Bucharest, and to a lesser extent, other towns like Constanta, Brasov and Timisoara. The jewel in Romania's crown is the region of Transylvania, which offers everything from skiing in the winter to walking, trekking, horse riding and a host of hospitable medieval towns and fortified villages surrounded by breathtaking natural beauty – although the property market in rural areas is extremely backward so proceed with caution.

The Balkans

How to buy

Romania has been amending its laws to lift all restrictions on foreign nationals owning land as well as property in the country – so far the law has only allowed foreign nationals to buy buildings, although this is set to change within five years of EU accession.

The way round this problem in the meantime – as in neighbouring Bulgaria – is to form a Romanian company and buy through that. As is the case anywhere, always engage the services of an English-speaking solicitor to represent your interests rather than relying on a notary.

Take particular care to properly set up the company through which you are buying the property.

As well as checking title, your lawyer may advise using a title insurance agent (as in Florida) as extra protection – and this may be useful as one of the legacies of Romania's life under the Ceaucescu regime, is the potential for ownership disputes.

At the signing of the promissory contract you will be expected to pay a deposit of 10-20%; completion must take place in front of a notary.

Costs

- **Estate agents' fees**: vary widely – check in advance
- **Legal fees**: allow 2%
- **Purchase taxes/fees**: allow 5% in total
- **VAT**: 19%
- **Capital gains/company profit tax when selling**: 16% (10% after two years)
- **Income tax on rental income**: 16% (expenses of 25% of takings are allowed as expenses)

Other information

- The Romanian government's website is at: www.gov.ro/engleza
- The British Embassy in Romania publishes a list of local lawyers. Visit www.britishembassy.gov.uk and follow the links.
- The website of the Romanian Embassy in the UK, www.roemb.co.uk, includes links to a range of useful organisations and government departments.
- British Romanian Chamber of Commerce: www.brcc-ccbr.org.
- Romanian Association of Real Estate Agents, www.arai.ro
- Romanian tourist board website: www.romaniatravel.com.

Eastern Europe

Historic, thriving cities, with a growing buy-to-let market.

In the period since the fall of the Berlin Wall in 1989 and the subsequent political upheavals across the countries of the former 'Eastern Bloc', a host of Eastern European nations have modernised and reformed their way into the European Union, and are now establishing themselves as competitive, westernised economies – with sustainable property markets to match.

Whilst countries like Hungary and Poland may not have traditionally been on the radar as popular holiday destinations for British tourists – partly on account of their climate and partly through simple ignorance of the delights they have to offer – the advent of the low cost airlines has opened up some of their most beautiful cities for year-round tourism.

At the same time, property law reforms have freed up foreigners to buy property, and in some cases land. Crucially, from an investment point of view, new-found competitiveness in countries as diverse as Estonia and Slovakia has not only helped foster burgeoning local property markets

but has also ushered in big business, creating a huge growth in demand for affordable property to rent and buy.

All the countries featured in this section joined the EU in 2004, so it could be argued that they are past their best in terms of ability to generate enormous capital growth in short spaces of time. But the gulf between property prices in all of them and their western equivalents is still, in places, huge – so buyers who choose wisely could still stand to make big gains.

Czech Republic

The property market

The Czech Republic – one of the 2004 entrants to the EU, and a country whose economy is gradually catching up with its western counterparts – is hilly and picturesque, and dotted with historic castles, romantic valleys and lakes, spas and ski slopes. The main attraction for overseas property buyers is the capital, Prague. Known as 'The City of One Hundred Towers and Spires', Prague has the kind of architectural heritage that is matched by few cities in the world; the centre, a UNESCO world heritage site, features a heady mix of Gothic, Functionalist, Art Deco, Art Nouveau and modern architecture. Beyond Prague, the river valleys of the Moldau and Elbe, and the region of southern Bohemia offer huge potential for buyers wanting a rural bolthole – although the real estate market in such areas is still geared up almost exclusively for domestic buyers.

How to buy

As in much of the formerly communist east, buying land (as distinct from buildings) in the Czech Republic is best achieved through setting up a company. Apart from this, the process is similar to what happens in many other countries, so the purchase follows the following pattern: limited due diligence; offer; preliminary contract (with deposit of 10% of purchase price); further due diligence; agreement of future purchase contract; purchase contract; and finally, cadastre registration. Registration in the land registry – the point at which ownership finally transfers to you – can take anything up to 6 months.

Costs

- **Estate agents' fees**: buyer may need to pay up to 3%
- **Legal fees including establishment of company**: allow 2–3%
- **Notary fees**: allow 1%
- **Mortgage fees**: 1% of amount borrowed
- **Real estate transfer tax** of 5% is payable by the seller, but by convention

the buyer pays it out of the total purchase price

- **VAT** on new build properties: 5%
- **Income tax** is progressive, with rates ranging from 15–32%; capital gains are taxed as income, although if the property is your main home you will be exempt if you have owned it for more than two years. Social security contributions for resident employees cost 12.5% of income.

Other information

- The FIABI-affiliated Czech Republic estate agents' association (*Asociace Realitních Kanceláří Ceske Republiky*) which has more than 200 members, is contactable on tel: +420 272 762953 or via www.arkcr.org.
- The official website of the Czech Republic is at www.czech.cz.
- *Home in the Czech Republic* is the title of a website aimed at anyone thinking about moving to the country: www.en.domavcr.cz/radyprozivot.shtml. It includes details on everything from education and working opportunities to social security contributions and how to get married or register births and deaths.
- The British Embassy in Prague lists English-speaking lawyers in the Czech Republic: go to www.britishembassy. gov.uk and follow the links.
- The Czech Chamber of Architects has a website at www.cka.cc.
- To find a range of professionals and business services, visit www.expats.cz/ directory.

Slovakia

The property market

The Slovak Republic has one of the fastest growing economies in Europe and several big employers, including Volkswagen, now have bases there. The capital city Bratislava, which lies on the Danube, close to the Austrian border, has been dubbed 'mini-Prague'. Many overseas buyers have bought new build and refurbished apartments there, both for long term and tourist lets. Elsewhere the countryside and villages of the High and Low Tatras mountain ranges are popular with holidaymakers all year round – and especially with skiers in the winter. The Liptov and Orava regions are also popular with tourists. Slovakia's under-supply of property relative to its burgeoning population makes the new-build market particularly active.

How to buy

Since joining the EU in 2004, Slovakia has relaxed its real estate laws, to allow foreigners to buy buildings and land – so it is no longer necessary to buy through a company. The buying process is similar to that in other western European countries, where the preliminary contract commits you to buy and a deposit of 20–30% of purchase price is expected. The usual rules of due diligence apply.

Buying costs

- **Estate agents' fees**: 5–10%; check upfront, because fees are often lumped into the initial purchase price
- **Real estate transfer tax**, which had been charged on a progressive scale from 6–20%, was abolished in 2005
- **Legal fees**: allow 2%
- **Mortgage arrangement fee**: 0.3%–1%
- **VAT**: 19% on new builds (within five years after the official completion of the construction) and land

Ongoing costs

Slovakia has a favourable tax regime, including a 19% flat rate of income tax.

Rental income is taxed at this rate, but you can deduct expenses, maintenance, property related costs, interest on any loans taken out to finance the property and even depreciation (spread out over 20 years).

Capital gains are taxed as income, but you are exempt if you own a property that you actually live in for two years; properties bought to rent out become exempt after five years. There is no inheritance tax in Slovakia.

There is a small real estate tax payable according to the property's size, specifications and location – but this generally costs less than a hundred pounds.

Other information

- Slovakia's National Association of Real Estate Agencies is part of CEREAN and has a website at www.narks-real.sk. It also operates an English language property search facility through www.reality.sk.
- The Slovak Chamber of Architects is at www.komarch.sk.
- The British Embassy in Bratislava has a list of English-speaking lawyers in Slovakia, visit www.britishembassy. gov.uk and follow the links. The Slovak Embassy in London has information about how to apply for residence in Slovakia, and links to relevant expat organisations in the UK. Visit www.slovakembassy.co.uk.
- The Slovak government website is at www.government.gov.sk/english
- The official tourist board website is at www.slovakiatourism.sk.
- Slovak Spectator, and English-language newspaper based in Slovakia has a website at www.slovakspectator.sk.

Hungary

The property market

A land-locked country in the heart of Europe, Hungary has stunning countryside and a beautiful capital city, Budapest – which is made up of two parts: Buda, with cobbled streets and medieval buildings, and Pest, the newer, commercial centre. Further up the Danube is the Carpathian Basin, which includes the tourist hotspots of Szentendre, Visegrad and Esztergom and to the south west of the capital is Lake Balaton – a highly prized second home destination.

How to buy

It is possible to buy property in Hungary as an individual, or to set up a company and buy through that. The chief disadvantage of buying as an individual is that you need to apply for government permission, which can take several months to be granted; buying as a company is quicker and confers tax advantages (see below), although it does commit you to more paperwork. Whichever route you take, make sure your lawyer checks the property's title carefully, clarifies that there are no debts attached and verifies that the building has been built legally.

Buying costs

- **Estate agents' fees**: allow 1.5–3%
- **Legal fees**: 1–2%
- **Stamp duty**: for a new build, the first €60,000 is exempt; the next €60,000 is charged at 6%; any amount above that is charged at 2%. For a resale property the first €16,000 is charged at 2% and any amount above this, at 6%. Companies which sell the property within two years may pay 2%
- **Company set-up costs**: allow at least £500.

Ongoing costs

- **Income tax**: If you buy as an individual, you must pay a flat rate of 20% income tax on rental income, with no allowances for expenses. If you buy as a company, you are allowed to offset expenses (including travel to the property as well as stamp duty, legal fees and the like) against the turnover, and pay only 16%.
- **Capital gains** are treated as income (although if you reinvest in Hungarian property within four years you can claim this tax back).
- **Local authority tax on land and buildings**: up to 3% of the market price per year
- **Inheritance tax**: on a progressive scale from 2.5%–21%, depending on the degree of relationship with the deceased.

Other information

- The Hungarian Real Estate Association, which is part of FIABCI and CEREAN, has a website at www.maisz.hu. As well as listing member agencies, the site includes a tariff showing how much agents may charge as commission, and for valuations.
- The British Embassy in Budapest keeps a list of English-speaking lawyers in Hungary. Visit www.britishembassy.gov.uk and follow the links.
- The Chamber of Hungarian Architects has a website at www.mek.hu
- Hungary's official website, with information about how the country's public services work, is at www.hungary.hu. The tourist board's website is at www.hungary.com.

Poland

The property market

By far the biggest country of the 2004 EU intake, Poland is in the grip of a long and far-reaching economic restructuring, which should ensure property prices continue to head upwards. Renovations and off-plan properties are frequently targeted at English-speaking buyers. The most popular location for British buyers is the historic city of Krakow – Poland's first 'city break' destination – but the capital, Warsaw, and other cities such as Poznan, Lodz and Lublin, also sell themselves as places offering good long term rental yields. Elsewhere, regions like Lubuskie on the German border and the Baltic coastal resorts of Gdansk, Sopot and Gdynia offer holiday home potential.

How to buy

As in most other countries, your lawyer should negotiate a preliminary contract, and you will need pay a deposit of between 10–30%; remaining searches and checks must take place before you sign the final deed in the presence of a notary. If you buy off-plan you may need to sign a reservation contract and pay a small deposit – which will be non-refundable. Your lawyer should insist on a suitable stage payment schedule and comprehensive guarantees.

Under Polish law you can buy property for investment purposes, or for your own use; although you may need to obtain permission from the Polish Interior Ministry if you are buying a holiday home (tel +48 22 6011870 or visit www.mswia.gov.pl). Your lawyer should be able to help you make an application; you should receive a 'permit promise' within a few months; this is valid for a year and is usually considered sufficient to proceed with the purchase because the permit cannot be refused while the promise is valid.

Buying costs

- **Estate agents' fees**: 6%, usually split 50/50 between buyer and seller
- **Legal fees**: allow 1–2%

- **Purchase tax** – 5% (2% if buying a shared ownership property)
- **Stamp duty**: 2%

Ongoing costs

- **Capital gains tax**: for foreign buyers there is a 10% tax on property that is resold within five years, unless the proceeds are invested in another Polish property
- **Income tax** has three thresholds, ranging from 19% to 40%, although it is possible to opt for a flat rate of 19% for 'business' income.
- Non-residents are not liable for **inheritance tax**.
- **Local authority real estate tax** is payable up to a maximum of less than 10 pence per square metre per year.

Other information

- The Polish Real Estate Federation, which is part of CEREAN, is contactable on tel +48 22 654 58 69 or via www.pref.org.pl.
- The British Embassy in Warsaw holds a list of English-speaking lawyers and sworn translators in Poland. Visit www.britishembassy.gov.uk and follow the links.
- The two representative bodies of architects are the National Chamber of Architects (www.izba architektow.pl) and the Union of Polish Architects (www.sarp.org.pl).
- The Polish Embassy in Dublin has published some advice for potential property investors, including contact details for estate agents. Visit www.dublin.polishembassy.ie/news1.htm.
- The Polish Information and Foreign Investment Agency provides help and guidance for people wanting to invest in Poland – including residential property buyers. The website is at http://paiz.gov.pl.
- The Polish government's website is at http://www.poland.gov.pl.
- The Polish Embassy in London is at www.polishembassy.org.uk.

Baltic States

Dynamic city break hotspots, off the beaten track.

Estonia

The property market

The main market is for apartments in the capital, Tallinn, bought by investors for long term or tourist lets. Foreigners can buy properties in Estonia freely, but have to apply for permission from the county governor to buy land; you have first refusal to buy the land, and permission is almost a formality if the land is less than 10 hectares.

Costs

Estate agents' fees, 2–6%; notary fees and stamp duty, allow several hundred pounds; legal fees, 1–2%; VAT, 18%; land tax 0.1–2.5% of market value of land annually; income/capital gains tax, 23%; no inheritance tax.

Other information

- British Embassy in Tallinn: www.britishembassy.gov.uk
- Chamber of Notaries: www.notar.ee
- The Estonian Law Centre: www.lc.ee
- The Parliament of Estonia: www.riigikogu.ee/?lang=en
- Estonian Embassy in London: www.estonia.gov.uk.
- Enterprise Estonia: www.investinestonia.com; UK office, tel 0207 838 5390
- Union of Estonian Architects: www.arhlitt.ee

 The British Embassies in Estonia, Latvia and Lithuania publish lists of English-speaking lawyers; the Latvian embassy also publishes lists of English-speaking doctors and translators. Visit www.britishembassy.gov.uk and follow the links.

Latvia

The property market

The capital, Riga, is a popular choice for investors, who buy apartments to rent out on a long-term basis, or to tourists. Off-plan properties are popular as developers usually only require a 10–15% deposit on reserving the property (this is held in an escrow account until completion); there are no staged payments and the balance is only payable on completion.

Costs

Estate agents' fees, 3–5%, VAT, 18% (0% if the property is more than a year old); mortgage arrangement fee, 0.5–1.0%; stamp duty, 2%; income tax, 25% flat rate (with generous expenses allowance); capital gains tax, 25% (0% on properties held for more than 12 months); council tax, 1.5% of the cadastral value of the property.

Other information

- Latvian Real Estate Association, tel +371 733 2034; www.lanida.lv
- Latvian Embassy in London: www.am.gov.lv
- Latvian Institute: www.li.lv
- Latvian Investment and Development Agency: www.liaa.gov.lv/eng/invest; UK office, tel 0207 229 8173
- Latvian Tourist Board: www.latviatourism.lv
- Latvian Chamber of Commerce: www.latvijas-talrunis.lv/lcci-new/index.htm
- Latvia Association of Architects: www.architektura.lv

Lithuania

The property market

As with its two closest neighbours, Lithuania's overseas property market centres on its capital city, Vilnius; although the government is also keen to attract investment in five other cities – Kaunas, Klaipeda, Siauliai, Panevezys and Elektrenai. Foreign buyers are able to buy properties without restriction, although to buy land involves gaining permission from the local municipality. Most land in Vilnius is owned by the state, so buyers own the property on a basis similar to leasehold in the UK and pay a ground rent.

Costs

Estate agents' fees, 2–5%; stamp duty, registration and notary fees: allow 3% in total; legal fees, 1–2%; VAT, 18%; real estate tax, 1%; income tax, 15%; capital gains tax, 15% (exempt after three years); inheritance tax, 5–10%, although close family members are exempt

Other information

- Lithuanian Real Estate Development Association, tel + 37 05 262 0350; www.lietuvosnt.lt.
- The Lithuanian land registry has a website at www.kada.lt
- The Lithuanian Development Agency website at www.lda.lt includes lists of estate agents and lawyers.
- For information on investing in Lithuania, visit www.development.lt
- Lithuanian Architects' Association: www.alas-architektai.lt/english/index.htm
- The Lithuanian Embassy in the UK: tel 0207 486 6401 or visit http://amb.urm.lt/jk/index.php?LangID=2.

Other destinations

If people want to visit or live there, it's a potential overseas property hotspot.

Europe

Although most British buyers look to the European countries featured earlier in this chapter when choosing an overseas property, the following nations also have their attractions:

Andorra

- **Property market**: Andorra has experienced high property price inflation and is popular with retirees; residents benefit from a very favourable tax regime. Around 10 million tourists visit every year, mainly to ski in the winter.
- **Find an agent**: *Collegi Professional d'Agents i Gestors Immobiliaris d'Andorra*, tel +376 80 11 15, www.agia.ad.

Austria

- **Property market**: Popular for skiing properties, especially around Innsbruck and the Salzburger region. Low cost airlines fly to Vienna, Salzburg and Graz.
- **Find an agent**: FIABCI-Österreich, tel +43 1 5127777, www.fiabci.at.

Benelux

- **Property market**: The region's property market has had mixed fortunes in recent years, with the Dutch boom tailing off while Belgium's price rises accelerate. The capital cities in particular offer buy-to-let potential.
- **Find an agent**: Belgium – *Confédération des Immobiliers de Belgique*, tel +32 9 22 20 622, www.cib.be; Netherlands – Dutch Association of Real Estate Brokers (*Nederlandse Vereniging van Makelaars*), tel +31 30 6085185, www.nvm.nl; Luxembourg – *Chambre Immobilière Du Grand Duché de Luxembourg*, tel +352 437475, www.cigdl.lu.

Germany

- **Property market**: Germany has the lowest owner-occupier rate of any EU country, but there are signs this is changing. Investors have been buying in Berlin and Frankfurt in the expectation of good long term capital growth. Purchase costs are high (around 11–12%).
- **Find an agent**: FIABCI-Deutschland, tel +49 40 4145 1616, www.fiabci.de; German Estate Agents' Association (*Immobilienverband Deutschland IVD Bundesverband*), tel +49 30 2757260, www.ivd.de.

Monaco

- **Property market**: Monaco is one of the most expensive – and reliable – places in the world to buy, and is expected to remain so thanks to its status as a tax haven.
- **Find an agent**: *Chambre Immobilière Monégasque*, tel +377 93509085, www.chambre-immo.monte-carlo.mc

Russia

- **Property market**: A small number of Russian and UK-based agents target foreign property investors, selling renovated and newly built properties in St Petersburg and Moscow, aimed mainly at buyers looking for a buy-to-let investment.
- **Find an agent**: The Russian Guild of Realtors has a website in Russian at www.rgr.ru.

Scandinavia

- **Property market**: Despite high standards of living, property in the Scandinavian countries is fairly cheap. Outside the main cities, population density is very low and the landscape stunning; holiday homes in coastal and mountain regions are popular.
- **Find an agent**: Denmark – Danish Association of Estate Agents (*Dansk Ejendomsmæglerforening*), tel +45 32 644 570, www.de.dk; Finland – FIABCI-Finland, tel +358 9 351 1155;

Finnish Real Estate Association, tel +358 9 530 8500, www.asuntoverkko.com; Norway – FIABCI-Norway, tel +47 22 053500, www.fiabci-norway.com; Sweden – FIABCI-Sweden, tel +46 8 342250; Association of Swedish Real Estate Agents, www.maklarsamfundet.se.

Switzerland

- **Property market**: Skiing and lake resorts, particularly around Geneva, attract retirees. Restrictions on foreign ownership, buying costs and taxes vary widely by canton.
- **Find an agent**: FIABCI-Suisse, tel +41 26 3505555, www.fiabci.ch; for German-speaking areas: *Schweizerischer Verband der Immobilienwirtschaft*, tel +41 1 4347888, www.svit.ch; for French-speaking areas: *Union Suisse des Professionnels de l'Immobilier*, tel +41 21 7963300, www.uspi.ch.

Ukraine

- **Property market**: Apartments in the capital, Kiev; holiday homes on the Black Sea coast (around Odessa) and in Carpathia. Some pundits predict gradual progress towards EU membership, making it a potential long-term investment prospect – but there are widely reported problems over establishing clear title.
- **Find an agent**: Ukrainian Realtors' Association, tel +38 0(44) 2066360, www.asnu.net/eng/index.html

Africa

Following the development of international tourism in several parts of Africa, adventurous British buyers have started to invest in property there too. The need for due diligence is even greater here than in emerging European markets, however, as estate agency is relatively unregulated, property title can be extremely difficult to clarify and financial and legal systems can be complex and unreliable.

Cape Verde

- **Property market**: Touted as the 'new Canaries' and the 'Caribbean on your doorstep', this 10-island archipelago, formerly a Portuguese colony, has been heavily promoted as the 'next big thing' for tourists and overseas property investors.
- **Useful contacts**: Look out for articles and advertisements from specific agents and developers in overseas property magazines. The Cape Verdian government has a website aimed at tourists and overseas investors, at http://virtualcapeverde.net.

Egypt

- **Property market**: There is plenty of activity centring on the Red Sea resorts of Sharm-el-Sheikh and Hurghada, with a mixture of English and local-based agents selling properties in resorts including Na'ama Bay, Dahab, Nuweiba, Taba Heights and El Gouna. Progress is slower on the Mediterranean coast.
- **Useful contacts**: Look out for articles and advertisements from specific agents

and developers in overseas property magazines. The British Embassy in Cairo publishes a list of English-speaking lawyers and official translators; visit www.britishembassy.gov.uk and follow the links.

Kenya

- **Property market**: New-build developments in resorts on Kenya's north east and southern coasts, like Malindi and Kilifi Creek, have attracted intrepid overseas buyers, as well as wealthy native second home owners.
- **Useful contacts**: Look out for articles and advertisements from specific agents and developers in overseas property magazines. Kenya High Commission, tel 0207 636 2371, www.kenya highcommission.com; Kenya National Chamber of Commerce and Industry, tel 00 25 420 228 016

Morocco

- **Property market**: A mixture of new-build developments and traditional riads have been tempting overseas buyers, with the regions around Marrakech, Tangier and Essaouria proving to be particular hotspots. The King of Morocco is keen to boost tourism across the country.
- **Useful contacts**: Look out for articles and advertisements from specific agents and developers in overseas property magazines. A guide to buying property in Morocco, and associated web forum, appears at www.buyingmoroccan property.com. The British Embassy in

211

Rabat publishes a list of English-speaking lawyers and official translators; visit www.british embassy.gov.uk and follow the links.

South Africa

- **Property market**: The most established of all the African property markets, South Africa has something to offer just about any kind of overseas buyer – from apartments and villas to townhouses, game reserves and development land.

Prices in the Cape region have been rising inexorably but there are still bargains to be found in many parts of the country.

- **Useful contacts**: Look out for articles and advertisements from specific agents and developers in overseas property magazines. South African Estate Agency Affairs Board, tel +27 11 731 5600, www.eaab.org.za. For a comprehensive guide on how to buy, visit www.pamgolding.co.za/advisory/advisory_nonsa residents.asp.

Asia

A range of Asian destinations have plenty to offer intrepid buyers who are in search of dream properties and are prepared to look further afield – but remember, the usual adage 'buyer beware' applies. Examples of locations growing in popularity include:

China

- **Property market**: Huge building programmes have been progressing in the major cities, especially Beijing. A small number of UK and China-based agents are selling residential investment properties that cost much less than their western equivalents, and hold out the prospect of regular income and long term capital growth. There are also UK companies offering property investment funds that buy Chinese residential property.
- **Find an agent**: Look out for particular companies advertising in overseas property magazines, or visit relevant websites, for example Beijing Lives,

which provides comprehensive real estate news and listings at www.beijinglives.com.

Dubai

- **Property market**: This tiny emirate – one of seven that make up the United Arab Emirates – sits on the Arabian Gulf Coast, surrounded by golden beaches and coral reefs. A Middle Eastern economic powerhouse, it has been wooing foreign investors with its combination of futuristic architecture (including the world's first man-made island, in the shape of a palm tree), theme parks, sporting activities and almost year-round sunshine.
- **Useful contacts**: Look out for articles and advertisements from specific agents and developers in overseas property magazines. The Dubai government's website is at www.dubai.ae/index.en.htm; the Chamber of Commerce has a site at

www.dcci.ae which includes a searchable online database. The British Embassy in the United Arab Emirates publishes a list of lawyers in the emirates, including Dubai.

Goa

- **Property market**: A former Portuguese colony, Goa is India's smallest state and a growing tourist destination benefiting from a tropical climate. Property prices are cheap by western standards, although the market is an immature one, with restrictions on foreign ownership and a complex inheritance system, leading to potential title problems.
- **Useful contacts**: Look out for articles and advertisements from specific agents and developers in overseas property magazines. Goa Tourist Board:

www.goatourism.org; a directory of real estate companies is at www.goarealestates.com.

Thailand

- **Property market**: Restrictions on foreign ownership mean buying as a company is common; developments in regions from Phuket and Koh Samui to Chiang Mai are marketed to overseas buyers.
- **Useful contacts**: Look out for articles and advertisements from specific agents and developers in overseas property magazines. Thailand Real Estate Broker Association +66 (0) 2285 4496-7; Thai Real Estate Association: +66 (0) 2229 3188 90, www.thairealestate.org; The Real Estate Broker Association: +66 (0) 2986 53889, www.reba.or.th.

The Americas

Argentina

- **Property market**: Undervalued properties in Buenos Aires, Patagonia and the Salta regions. Purchase costs can reach more than 25% of asking price if you are buying in a new development.
- **Find an agent**: Follow the link from the International Consortium of Real Estate Associations (www.worldproperties.com) or visit The Argentina Chamber of Horizontal Properties and Real Estate Activities, www.caphai.com.ar. The Buenos Aires International Newcomers group is a virtual community based at http://groups.yahoo.com/group/buenosairesinternationalnewcomers.

Brazil

- **Property market**: Still very much an emerging market, most of the action is in the north eastern Bahia region (main city, Salvador) although properties in resorts around Fortaleza – Brazil's fifth largest city and the capital of Ceara state – are also attracting interest.
- **Find an agent**: Look out for articles and advertisements from specific agents and developers in overseas property magazines. Find an agent: FIABCI-Brasil, tel +55 11 50787778, www.fiabcibrasil.com.br.

213

Canada

- **Property market:** The second largest country in the world, Canada is a perennial favourite for British émigrés, and in recent years developers have been targeting UK buyers with everything from chic Toronto apartments to ranch-style properties in Manitoba and log cabins in the ski resorts of British Columbia.
- **Find an agent:** Look out for articles and advertisements from specific agents and developers in overseas property magazines. FIABCI-Canada, tel +1 905 337 2546, www.fiabci-canada.com; The Canadian Real Estate Association, tel +1 613 2377111, www.crea.ca.

The Caribbean Islands

- **Property market:** Islands with property markets already popular, or gaining in popularity, among overseas investors include Anguilla, Antigua, Barbados, Cayman Islands, Dominican Republic, St Kitts and Nevis and the Turks and Caicos Islands. A huge range of property is available, from crumbling beach shacks to five-star marina-style resorts. Mainland countries with Caribbean coastlines, including Belize and Costa Rica, may also have investment potential.
- **Find an agent:** There is no pan-Caribbean estate agency body but individual countries' groups include the Bahamas Real Estate Association, www.bahamas realestateassociation.com, and the Association of Real Estate Agents of Trinidad and Tobago, http://community.wow.net/area/HOME.HTM. Look out for individual agents' or developers' details in magazines and on the internet; there are also collective websites representing agencies on more than one island, including the Caribbean Property List, www.caribpro.com; and www.caribbean realestate showcase. com. Individual embassies or consulates, accessible through www.britishembassy.gov.uk, may be able to assist with lists of English-speaking lawyers, or general property buying advice.

Mexico

- **Property market:** As Mexico has slowly established itself as a tourist destination, it has also loosened its property laws, which has allowed foreigners – mainly from the US, but also some from the UK, to buy property in non-border areas.
- **Find an agent:** Look out for articles and advertisements from specific agents and developers in overseas property magazines. For a guide to buying in Mexico, see www.mexperience.com/property/default.htm. FIABCI-Mexico, tel +52 5 5664260, www.fiabci.com.mx; *Asociación Mexicana de Profesionales Inmobiliarios*, www.ampidf.com.mx.

Panama

- **Property market:** With natural beauty and sunny days aplenty, Panama is marketing itself hard as an international retirement destination, thanks to its generous *Pensionado* Programme.
- **Useful contacts:** Look out for articles and advertisements from specific agents and developers in overseas property magazines. For details of the *Pensionado* Programme, contact the Panama Consulate at www.panaconsul.com.
- **Find an agent:** *Asociación Panameña de Corredores y Promotores de Bienes Raíces*, tel +507 2287840, www.acobir.com

214

United States

- **Property market**: Outside Florida, estate agents in a host of locations across the US are now marketing properties to overseas buyers. Areas already popular, or growing in popularity, include New England (the states of Massachusetts, Connecticut, Rhode Island, Vermont, New Hampshire and Maine), where you can buy everything from archetypal clapperboard homes with sea or lake frontage to smaller bungalows and log cabins; Las Vegas, where new and resale condominium homes sell well; California; Seattle; the Virginias; and North and South Carolina.

- **Find an agent in the US**: FIABCI-USA, tel +1 703 5244279, www.fiabci-usa.com; National Association of Realtors, tel + 800/874-6500, or visit http://www.realtor.org/leadrshp.nsf/webassoc?OpenView and search for members by state; Association of Foreign Investors in Real Estate – a networking organisation which provides useful information and discussion forums for overseas investors, tel +1 202 312 1400, www.afire.org.

Australasia

Popular with British émigrés and retirees for decades, Australia and New Zealand offer wide open spaces and – outside the most fashionable urban districts – affordable property prices for British buyers who can get past the tough immigration rules and cope with living thousands of miles away from the UK.

Australia

- **Useful contacts**: Real Estate Institute of Australia, tel +61 2 62824277, www.reia.com.au; British High Commission in Canberra: http://bhc.britaus.net; Australian Department of Immigration and Multicultural Affairs: www.immi.gov.au.

New Zealand

- **Useful contacts**: Real Estate Institute of New Zealand, www.reinz.co.nz; Overseas Investment Office www.oio.linz.govt.nz; British High Commission in Wellington, follow the links from www.britishembassy.gov.uk.

Useful addresses

Professional and regulatory bodies

Architects' Council of Europe
Rue Paul Emile Janson, 29
B-1050 Brussels, Belgium
Tel: 00 32 2 543 11 40
Website: www.ace-cae.org

Association of Independent Financial Advisers
Austin Friars House, 2-6 Austin Friars
London EC2N 2HD
Tel: 020 7628 1287
Website: www.aifa.net

Association of Independent Property Professionals
Website: www.aipp.org.uk

Confederation Europeenne d'Immobilier
VBO (CEI) - P/Box 17330
2502 CH - The Hague, Netherlands
Tel: 00 31 70 345 87 03
Website: www.web-cei.com

Conseil des Notariats de l'Union Européenne
Avenue de Cortenbergh, 52
B - 1000 Brussels, Belgium
Tel: 00 32 2 513 95 29
Website: www.cnue.be (French)

Federation of Overseas Property Developers, Agents and Consultants
First Floor, 618 Newmarket Road
Cambridge CB5 8LP
Tel: 0870 3501223
Website: www.fopdac.com

Financial Services Authority
25 The North Colonnade, Canary Wharf
London E14 5HS
Tel: 020 7066 1000
www.fsa.gov.uk

Financial Ombudsman Service
South Quay Plaza
183 Marsh Wall, London E14 9SR
Tel: 0845 080 1800 or 020 7964 1000
www.financial-ombudsman.org.uk

Independent Financial Adviser Promotion
2nd Floor, 117 Farringdon Rd
London EC1R 3BX
Tel: 020 7833 3131
www.unbiased.co.uk

International Real Estate Federation (FIABCI)
FIABCI Secretariat, 23 avenue Bosquet
75007 Paris, France
Tel: 00 33 1 4550 4549
Website: www.fiabci.org

Law Society of England and Wales
Law Society Hall, 113 Chancery Lane
London WC2A 1PL
Tel: 020 7242 1222
Website: www.lawsociety.org.uk

Organisation for Timeshare in Europe
Oak House, Cours St. Michel 100/3
B-1040 Brussels, Belgium
Website: www.ote-info.com
Royal Institute of British Architects
66 Portland Place, London W1B 1AD
Tel: 020 7580 5533
www.architecture.com or www.riba.org

Royal Institution of Chartered Surveyors
Surveyor Court, Westwood Way
Coventry CV4 8JE
Tel: 0870 333 1600
Website: www.rics.org

UK/EU government bodies
The Pension Service
International Pension Centre
Tyneview Park, Benton
Newcastle–upon–Tyne NE98 1BA
Tel: 0191 218 7777
www.thepensionservice.gov.uk or
www.dwp.gov.uk

European Commission FIN–NET
http://europa.eu.int/comm/internal_mark
et/finservices–retail/index_en.htm.

European Employment Services
Tel: 008 00 4080 4080 (free phone) or
00 32 16 271 216
Website: www.europa.eu.int/eures

Foreign and Commonwealth Office
Old Admiralty Building
London SW1A 2PA
Tel: 0207 008 1500 or 0207 008
0218 (services for Britons overseas)
www.fco.gov.uk

HM Revenue and Customs Centre for
Non–Residents
Tel: 0845 070 0040 (or 00 44 151
210 2222) for income/capital gains tax;
0845 9 154811 (or 00 44 191 203
7010) for national insurance
www.hmrc.gov.uk/cnr

Consumer bodies
The Citizen's Advice Bureaux'
European Consumer Centre
PO Box 3308
Wolverhampton WV10 9ZS
Website: www.euroconsumer.org.uk

Timeshare Consumers' Association
Hodsock, Worksop
Nottinghamshire S81 0TF
Tel: 01909 591 100
Website: www.timeshare.org.uk
Email: info@timeshare.org.uk

Which?
Castlemead, Gascoyne Way
Hertford SG14 1LH
Tel: 0800 252100
Website: www.which.co.uk

Sources for emigrants
British Association of Removers
Tangent House, 62 Exchange Road
Watford, Hertfordshire WD18 0TG
Tel: 01923 699480
Website: www.bar.co.uk

Council of International Schools
21A Lavant Street, Petersfield
Hampshire GU32 3EL
Tel: 01730 263131
www.cois.org

Department of Health
Richmond House, 79 Whitehall
London SW1A 2NS
Tel: 020 7210 4850
www.dh.gov.uk

European Network of National
Information Centres on academic
recognition and mobility
www.enic–naric.net

Fédération Internationale des
Déménageurs Internationaux
Website: www.fidi.com

Overseas Moving Network International
Website: www.omnimoving.com

217

Index

Page numbers in bold type indicate the main entry for a country.

which?

Which? is the leading independent consumer champion in the UK. A not-for-profit organisation, we exist to make individuals as powerful as the organisations they deal with in everyday life. The next two pages give you a taster of our many products and services. For more information, log onto www.which.co.uk or call 0800 252 100.

Which? magazine

Which? is, quite simply, the most trusted magazine in the UK. It takes the stress out of your buying decisions by offering independent, thoroughly researched advice on consumer goods and services from cars to current accounts via coffee makers. Its Best Buy recommendations are the gold standards in making sound and safe purchases across the nation. Which? has been making things happen for all consumers since 1957 – and you can join us by subscribing at www.which.co.uk or calling 0800 252 100 and quoting 'Which'.

Which? online

www.which.co.uk gives you access to all Which? content online. Updated daily, you can read hundreds of product reports and Best Buy recommendations, keep up to date with Which? campaigns, compare products, use our financial planning tools and interactive car-buying guide. You can also access all the reviews from the *The Which? Good Food Guide*, ask an expert in our interactive forums, register for e-mail updates and browse our online shop – so what are you waiting for? www.which.co.uk.

Holiday Which?

Full of independent and unbiased travel advice, *Holiday Which?* gives you the lowdown on insurance, tour operators and holiday health, as well as the know-how to avoid rip-offs and get compensation when it's due. That's not all – the magazine also contains information on the best short breaks, long-haul trips and fun days out, recommending good places to stay and eat. To find out more about *Holiday Which?* log on to www.which.co.uk or call 0800 252 100 and quote 'Holiday'.

which?

Which? Books

Which? Books provides impartial, expert advice on everyday matters from finance to law, property to major life events. We also publish the country's most trusted restaurant guide, *The Which? Good Food Guide.* To find out more about Which? Books, log on to www.which.co.uk or call 01903 828557.

Other books in this series

Which? Essential Guides
Buy, Sell and Move House
Kate Faulkner
ISBN: 1-84490-026-6/978-1844-900-268

A complete, no-nonsense guide to negotiating the property maze and making your move as painless as possible. From dealing with estate agents to chasing solicitors, working out the true cost of your move to understanding Home Information Packs, this guide tells you how to keep things on track and avoid painful sticking points.

Which? Essential Guides
The Pension Handbook
Jonquil Lowe
ISBN: 1-844900-25-8/978-1844-900-251

A definitive guide to sorting out your pension, whether you're deliberating over SERPs/S2Ps, organising a personal pension or moving schemes. Cutting through confusion and dispelling apathy, Jonquil Lowe provides up-to-date advice on how to maximise your savings and provide for the future.

“Which? tackles the issues that really matter to consumers and gives you the advice and active support you need to buy the right products.”